Moses—The Prince, the Prophet

Moses
The Prince, the Prophet

HIS LIFE, LEGEND

& MESSAGE FOR OUR LIVES

RABBI LEVI MEIER, Ph.D.

JEWISH LIGHTS PUBLISHING
Woodstock, Vermont

Moses—The Prince, the Prophet:
His Life, Legend & Message for Our Lives

1999 First Quality Paperback Edition

Library of Congress Cataloging-in-Publication Data

    Moses—the prince, the prophet : his life, legend
  & message for our lives / by Levi Meier.
      p.   cm.
  Includes bibliographical references.
  ISBN 1-58023-013-X (Hardcover)
  ISBN 1-58023-069-5 (Quality Paperback)

    1. Moses (Biblical leader)   I. Title.
BS580.M6M36   1998
222'.1092—dc21
[b]   98-35473
                                      CIP

10 9 8 7 6 5 4 3 2 1

Manufactured in the United States of America

Jacket art: *The Burning Bush* of the Gates of Sinai Suite
by Shraga Weil, 1991. Available from the Safrai Gallery,
19 King David St., Jerusalem, 94101, Israel.
Fax: 972-2-6240387.

Jacket design: Kieran McCabe
Text design: Terry Bain

Published by Jewish Lights Publishing
A Division of LongHill Partners, Inc.
Sunset Farm Offices, Route 4
P.O. Box 237
Woodstock, VT 05091
Tel: (802) 457-4000
Fax: (802) 457-4004
www.jewishlights.com

IN MEMORY OF MY BELOVED GRANDPARENTS,

Emily and Moritz Heiser
Clara and Julius Meier

Contents

Acknowledgments

FIRST AND FOREMOST, I want to thank DreamWorks SKG, whose animated film project *The Prince of Egypt* inspired me to explore the life of Moses. Steven Spielberg, Jeffrey Katzenberg, and David Geffen showed tremendous foresight in examining the life of this remarkable man whose mission changed the course of human history. In particular, I want to acknowledge the role of Jeffrey Katzenberg, who took his studio's project from concept to reality.

Special gratitude and appreciation to my dear friend Paula R. Van Gelder for her ever-present readiness and expertise in preparing the material and editing this book.

I also want to thank those wise and learned individuals who critically and meticulously read my manuscript before publication. I am indebted to Manfred Altman, Kenneth M. Chasen, Lone Jensen, Fred Rosner, and my dear brother and sister-in-law, Rabbi Menahem and Tzipora Meier, for their valuable comments. I am most grateful to Uriela Obst, who assisted me with her expert suggestions about the content of this work. I would also like to thank my agent, Alan Nevins of Renaissance, for his dedication and diligent efforts on my behalf.

I want to thank Stuart Matlins, publisher of Jewish Lights Publishing, for his wholehearted support of this project. He and his staff have carefully guided this work through the publication process. In particular, I want to acknowledge Editorial Director Arthur J. Magida's meticulous attention to detail in reviewing this manuscript. Associate Editor Jennifer P. Goneau was extremely helpful and conscientious in all her important work on this book.

I have dedicated this volume to my beloved grandparents, one of whom, Julius Meier, lived with us when I was a child. I have wonderful memories of him walking me to Hebrew school and peeling apples and oranges for me. My dear mother, Mrs. Frieda Meier, continues to be a source of inspiration to me.

My dear family continues to be the focus of my life. I wish to express my love to my wife Marcie and our children. They make my life a blessing.

Introduction

I gets weary and sick of tryin'
I'm tired of livin', and scared of dyin'. . .
—"Ol' Man River" from *Showboat*

IT'S NO SURPRISE that these lyrics continue to touch people's hearts some seventy years after they were written. After all, not that much about life has changed. Certainly, there have been a lot of developments in the world since 1927. Computers, faxes, e-mail, and cellular phones, for instance, may now dominate our lives. But we, as *people*, have not changed much at all.

Perhaps that is why the stories of the ancients continue to intrigue and inspire us as we search for meaning in our own lives. Just as they had fears and hopes and aspirations, so do we. Just as they entered into relationships, so do we. Just as they experienced birth and death, love and loss, so do we. And just as they were enslaved, so are we, although perhaps not in the same way.

The saga of the Israelites' Exodus from Egypt is the greatest story of liberation from enslavement ever told. It is a metaphor for all people and all times. As we approach the year 2000 and the next millennium, it becomes increasingly clear that each of us needs to be released from our own forms of enslavement. We may not work at forced labor as the Israelites did, but we certainly need help in leaving our own personal "Egypts." By that, I mean the narrow straits of our own existence—the meaninglessness, depression, anxiety, neuroses, and addictions that too often govern our lives.

Certainly, our days can contain many joyful and meaningful moments. Yet there are certain circumstances in our lives that we know we cannot escape. We were born and we will die. In between, we often experience pain and illness, both physical and emotional. And we will experience most of our suffering alone. It is no wonder that we spend so much time looking for quick ways to ease our pain—rushing from one relationship to another, seeking relief in intimacy with another person, or trying to drown our sorrows in alcohol, sex, drugs, or food. All these outlets are essentially ways of self-medicating ourselves to alleviate the pain that we experience as part of the human condition.

Some of us seek healthier ways to make it through life—relationships, hobbies, creative drives, friendship, and humor. Some of us look to trusted friends or relatives, physicians, therapists, or clergy. We choose our advisors from among those who seem to have found their own ways to struggle and cope successfully.

But is there one person from history whom we can all turn to, whose life provides profound examples of how personal struggle against terrible odds can bring about liberation and change? I think there is. He is the biblical Moses. He is central to Judaism, Christianity, and Islam, as well as to many other religions of the world. He lived 3,200 years ago, and grew up as a pampered prince in Egypt, only to abandon the palace life to become a humble shepherd. Ultimately, he was destined to become the greatest leader of humanity.

THE PROMISED LAND AWAITS US ALL

When most people study Moses, they look at him in terms of the stories about him that they learned in childhood. Moses's life, like ours, was not easy. He experienced pain, difficulties, and failures.

For the first three months of his life, he could not even cry out loud lest he be discovered and killed. His mother silenced him every time he reacted normally to hunger, discomfort, fatigue, or fear. After those three months, he was placed in a basket on a river, with an uncertain destiny waiting for him around the bend.

Moses actually had two mothers—a biological mother who gave birth to him, and an adoptive mother who helped save his life and then raised him. Moses grew up in the court of the pharaoh, but he was mindful that the enslaved Hebrews (also known as Israelites) were, in reality, his brethren. He faced many other challenges, not the least of which was a severe stutter.

Then, in his eightieth year, something happened to Moses that would change him, as well as the entire course of human history. He climbed a mountain in the desert, Mount Sinai. We will never know exactly what happened to him there, but when he came down, he told the people who were with him that God had given him the answer to every question about life that he had, that they had, and that their descendants would have. And the people were awed.

Moses told his people that if they listened carefully and did what he taught them, they would understand the meaning of life. The words that Moses recorded continue to help each of us find purpose and direction today.

For Jews, the Five Books of Moses that he received from God at Sinai are the Torah, which Christians regard as an integral part of their Bible. Some of Islam's teachings are similar to precepts of the Torah. So it is a most important book to an immense segment of humanity, given to help lead us from oppression to freedom, from depression to joy. It was meant to guide each of us on our individual journey to the Promised Land, which awaits us all. But the Promised Land is not just the physical place, flowing with milk and honey, to which Moses led two or three million people after they were liberated from Egypt. It is a metaphor for a better, more meaningful and joyful life.

Moses's story encompasses much more than the biography of an individual. His life is intertwined with the story of a people: the Israelites' Exodus from Egypt, the birth of a new nation, and the Divine revelation at Mount Sinai. The events in Moses's life are inseparable from the great mission for which he was chosen. In this book, I try to understand Moses's experiences in contemporary terms, based on my perspective as a rabbi, hospital chaplain, and clinical psychologist. I use numerous examples drawn from real life—primarily from the lives of people who have been my clients, patients, and students. I hope that their experiences make Moses's teachings more relevant to you.

FINDING COMFORT IN THE VOICE OF GOD

As we explore the biblical stories of Moses's life and work, you will note that I use translations from the Hebrew text to explain and amplify those points that I find significant. Also, I refer often to the Midrash, the Jewish oral tradition that was written down about 2,000 years ago. The stories of the Midrash offer much insight into the human side of biblical characters, and they effectively teach us about interpersonal dynamics, then and now.

My purpose in all of this is to show that all of us—despite the circumstances of our birth and the life we have lived thus far—can be leaders and help bring others out of the slavery of everyday addiction or oppression. And by helping to save others, we will actually save ourselves.

As the Talmud states, "He who saves even one life has saved the whole world." So set yourself a small task. Do not aim to save the whole world. Save one life. Save yourself. It will be as if you saved the entire world. By saving one person in your family or in the entire family of humanity *you* can be the next Moses.

As you set about this task, take comfort in the knowledge that the Voice that spoke to Moses from atop Mount Sinai—the Voice that proclaimed, "I am the Eternal your God, Who brought you out of the land of Egypt, out of the house of bondage"—has never ceased. It continues to reverberate to this day. You can hear that Voice as you listen to the yearnings of your soul.

And as you think about the difficult aspects of your life, you may be comforted by the words once spoken to me by a patient whom I used to visit during her frequent hospitalizations for treatment of a chronic illness. This forty-five-year-old single mother of two teenage daughters had worked for many years as an elementary school teacher. But her real passions were her creative writing and art appreciation classes. As we got to know each other, she read some of her poetry to me, and I found it to be insightful and meaningful. I was particularly impressed when I realized how much poetry she wrote when she was in acute pain.

During one of her hospitalizations, it became clear that her condition was terminal and that she would not be going home. As I entered her room one day, I saw her speaking into a small tape recorder. She momentarily stopped her recording and turned to me, explaining that she was preparing special tapes for each of her daughters—to be listened to on their wedding days and on the day that each would hopefully give birth to a child.

It was clear that this exceptional woman was leaving a very special legacy. When I visited her for the last time, she took my hand in hers and said to me softly, "It's all been worthwhile because of the love and the poetry and the art. Life has really been a gift." It is my hope, dear reader, that by understanding the life of Moses, you too will have a chance to discover the gift of your own life.

PART I

Overcoming All Odds

CHAPTER 1

The Birth of a Hero

H E WAS A TINY BABY BOY placed in a basket and sent floating to his destiny down the river Nile.

When most of us think about the beginning of Moses's life,
that is the image that comes to mind. But that is not the way that
his story, as told in the book of Exodus, begins. It starts with a
very simple statement, so short that we tend to skip over it as we
hurry on to the next part of the text: "And there went a man of
the house of Levi, and he took to wife a daughter of Levi."

At first glance, this appears to be just an ordinary description
of the marriage of two people. But it is more than that. We know
from other biblical references that Moses's parents had been married for some time and already had two other children, Miriam
and Aaron. So why does this puzzling verse sound as if the
parents—Amram and Yocheved—were newlyweds?

To understand what is going on, we must take a look at the
larger canvas of the life of the Israelites in ancient Egypt.

The year, as near as we can tell, is 1200 B.C.E. The Egyptian
empire is at its height. The pyramids and the sphinx are already
standing. The Israelites had come there hundreds of years earlier
during a great famine. The Egyptians had survived this trying

time thanks to the visions of Joseph, who, after being sold into slavery by his brothers, became an advisor to the pharaoh. Joseph, whose father was the Hebrew patriarch Jacob, successfully interpreted the pharaoh's dreams, explaining that they meant that Egypt would experience seven years of abundant crops, to be followed by seven years of famine. Joseph advised that during the time of "feast," storehouses should be built and stocked for the years of famine. The pharaoh followed Joseph's advice and Egypt was saved.

During this time, Joseph's brothers, who were starving, came to Egypt to buy food. Joseph recognized them, forgave them, and brought all the sons of Jacob and their families to live in Egypt.

At the time that Moses's story begins, Joseph had already died. The Israelite population had increased dramatically, and they were seen as a growing threat to the Egyptians.

The new pharaoh—probably Ramses II—chooses not to remember the contributions of Joseph or any debt he might owe to Joseph's descendants. Instead, he enslaves the Israelites.

Yet the deprivations and persecutions seem to make no difference to the Israelites, who continue to flourish and multiply. The pharaoh grows paranoid. These people threaten his power base.

At this time, the pharaoh's soothsayers and magicians bring him even more disquieting news. According to the stars, the Israelites will one day defeat Egypt. A savior is about to be born to them who will free the slaves and cause havoc in Egypt.

The pharaoh trembles. He wants the Israelites to keep building the magnificent cities of Ramses and Pithom. And he wants to be able to control them.

The magicians have a solution. The stars seem to indicate that the designated savior of the Israelites is vulnerable to water. If all the newborn Israelite males were drowned, surely the savior would perish as well. And thus an edict is issued from the palace: "Every son that is born you shall cast into the river."

The Israelites weep and moan as they see newborn boys being

drowned daily. Amram and Yocheved, the parents of two children, separate. They will not bring a new life into the world to see it destroyed. It is easier to be apart than to risk something so terrible.

Children always hate divorce. And Miriam, the eldest daughter, feels that she is a victim of her parents' desperate decision. Her intuition tells her that everything about this is wrong.

She argues with her parents. "Your decision is harsher than that of the pharaoh!" she says. "Are you not killing your unborn child? Perhaps it would have been a girl—it could have lived! The pharaoh may or may not put the newborn to death, but you have made certain it cannot live."

REMEMBERING GOD'S PROMISE

Thus, a little girl shamed her parents into reuniting after three years. *This* is where our story begins. Amram and Yocheved reunite. "And there went a man of the house of Levi, and he took to wife a daughter of Levi. "

They decided to try again. And yet, what were they about to do? How could an Israelite couple make love, risking death for a child they might conceive? A son would be doomed to certain death. Even a daughter might be raped by Egyptian soldiers. How could they even think of adding to their family? This issue is similar to what I hear today from young couples I counsel who are reluctant to bring new life into a world of pain and suffering.

But that is *exactly* the point that the Bible is trying to get across to us. Even in the midst of trouble, despair, and danger, we can choose to be life-affirming. And the most life-affirming act of all is to bring another life into this world, because if we stop to think about it, *whenever* we bring new life into this world, we—as the only species that is aware of our own mortality—also consciously bring inevitable death into the world. That is a very frightening and sobering thought. Additionally, we are cognizant of all the pain inherent in life itself—illness, emotional suffering, financial hardships, betrayal, the difficulties of even normal aging, separation, and loss. Yet, despite this knowledge of what lies ahead for our children, most of us still choose to bring new life into the world. There are many reasons for such a decision. For some, it is the profound desire to propagate, to continue the species, the family line, or the societal group. For others, it may be the desire to achieve immortality by living through children and grandchildren. Continuity of society as a whole may also be a consideration. Psychoanalyst Erik Erikson, who traced the stages of human psychosocial development, describes this drive as "generativity"—a vital interest outside of the home in establishing and guiding the next generation or in bettering society.

Ultimately, though, giving birth is a declaration that love is stronger than death. Having a baby affirms that life and death are part of a Divine plan. Our all-too-human side may tell us that there is little reason to reproduce. But our Higher Self, the Divine element within us, gives us the strength, the will, and the desire to continue.

For Amram and Yocheved—the father and mother of Moses— the decision to have a child was not simple. According to the Midrash, on the one hand, they remembered God's promise to Abraham, Isaac, and Jacob that the people of Israel would continue to grow, thrive, and settle eventually in the Promised Land. On the other hand, they were faced with the harsh reality of a genocidal edict: the pharaoh was intent on killing all newborn males.

Confronted with the physical dangers of Egypt, Amram and Yocheved were first afraid to bring another child into the world. However, even though their daughter Miriam was young, she was blessed with prophetic vision. She went to her parents and told them what she had foreseen: "This time, a son will be born to my father and my mother, and he will save the Israelites from the hand of Egypt."

Amram heeded the Divine promise rather than surrender to his personal fears. He returned to his wife, hence the biblical reference to their reunion as if they were newlyweds. Shortly thereafter, Moses was conceived.

But there is yet another puzzle in this opening verse. Amram and Yocheved are not referred to by name at this crucial moment. We are simply told, "And there went a man of the house of Levi, and he took to wife a daughter of Levi. And the woman conceived and bore a son." In the original Hebrew, the word for man is *ish*, and for woman, *isha*.

In other instances, *ish* and *isha* describe angels or individuals who are sent on a special, Divine mission to help fulfill a particular destiny.

Moses's father and mother were such an *ish* and *isha*. They had a special mission to fulfill: conceiving a child who would one day lead the Israelites out of Egypt and to the Promised Land. Was the Divine mission of Moses's parents unique? Or can their story parallel our own lives as well?

The great medieval philosopher Maimonides wrote that every human being has the potential to be as righteous as Moses. To me, this means that just as Miriam foresaw that Moses would save his people, so too can every newborn child be regarded as a potential hero—a potential savior of humanity at some time to come. For, as the Talmud explains, there are three partners in the creation of every child—God, the mother, and the father.

But before Moses could grow to adulthood and fulfill his mission, his mother would have to rescue him from the edict of the pharaoh. Ironically, she would save him from being drowned in the river Nile by placing him in the very same river. It is this watery journey that we shall explore next.

CHAPTER 2

The Daughter of God

MOSES'S BIRTH WAS TRYING and dangerous. He was born in a country that did not want him, and at a time when the pharaoh had issued a genocidal decree: "Every son that is born you shall cast into the river."

Thousands of babies were murdered, yet Yocheved managed to hide her newborn son. But by the time Moses was three months old, Yocheved knew she could not safely keep him at home any longer. So she lovingly fashioned a basket out of bulrushes, coated it with pitch, and set it among the reeds near the bank of the river Nile. She would sneak out at night to nurse her son, and during the day, Moses's sister Miriam was given the responsibility of standing nearby to guard the infant, making sure that no harm befell him.

Then a most amazing thing happened. The pharaoh's daughter came down to bathe in the river, saw the tiny basket near the reeds, and ordered her servants to retrieve it. This daughter of the very pharaoh who was plotting Moses's death was the one who saved him.

At first glance, the biblical text does not seem to tell us a lot about the pharaoh's daughter, yet it actually tells us everything.

In the biblical book of Chronicles and in the Midrash, we learn that the name of the Egyptian princess was *Bitya*, meaning—of all things—"Daughter of God"!

Astonishing! None of the great matriarchs or other wise women in the Bible were given such a holy name. But this woman—the daughter of the murderous pharaoh—was granted this special distinction. Can you imagine the daughter of Hitler or Stalin or another tyrant being called such a name?

Obviously, we are being told something very important here, something that carries important implications today.

I believe that we can derive two central lessons from this story about Moses's two mothers—Yocheved, who was a God-fearing monotheist, and Bitya, who worshiped idols. First, we learn that we should never make assumptions about people. Whatever we might know about someone's family, religion, or ethnicity is not as significant as that person's *ethical character*. Secondly, the Torah tells us that Divine revelation pertains to all people, and that ultimately there are only two "races"—people who are primarily good, and those who are essentially evil.

TEARS OF COMPASSION

So these are the lessons of Bitya's very special, holy name. And the biblical description of her actions helps explain what she did to deserve that designation: "And she opened it [the basket], and she saw him, the child; and behold a boy that was weeping. And she had compassion on him, and she said: 'This is one of the Hebrews' children.'"

Somehow, the reality of seeing that helpless, crying infant elicited compassion in Bitya, wiping out any hatred that had been instilled in her for the Israelites. Her father's decree had seemed to be a general edict about a hypothetical people who were completely unreal to her. But here was a real, crying Hebrew baby who needed to be nurtured, and whose tears moved Bitya to shed her own tears.

Once Bitya rescued the infant, Miriam came forward from where she had been hiding and approached the pharaoh's daughter, offering to provide a Hebrew woman to serve as a wet nurse for the infant. When Bitya agreed to this proposal, Miriam, of course, simply got Yocheved. When the baby was finally weaned, Yocheved brought him back to Bitya, who adopted him and gave him the name "Moses." Presumably, this comes from the Egyptian word *munyos* or the Hebrew verb *mashoh,* both of which mean "to draw out." As Bitya bestowed the name, she explained, "I drew him out of the water." Water, as we will eventually see, will become one of the recurring themes of Moses's life.

When Bitya rescued Moses from the water, she truly earned the name "daughter of God." She disobeyed her father, who was the supreme ruler over all of Egypt, and probably risked her own life. But more significantly, she demonstrated that she had reached the highest stage of human moral development. She made her decision based on considerations of the greater good, of the proper, ethical thing to do for humanity in general, rather than for her own family.

Psychologist Lawrence Kohlberg of the Center for Moral Development at Harvard studied the evolution of moral judgment and moral action. He asserted that selfless behavior, such as that demonstrated by Bitya, reflects the highest level of moral development. This occurs when our concern for others takes precedence over self-interest or social values.

The Midrash tells us that Moses's tears were incredibly powerful in affecting Bitya's emotions and behavior. To me, tears are the body's natural system for purification and spiritual catharsis. It is important to remember, as the sages teach us, that the gates of heaven can always be opened through prayers accompanied by tears.

In *When Nietzsche Wept,* psychiatrist Irving Yalom explains the power of tears, noting that sometimes the process of psychotherapy goes along for weeks and months with no discernible progress. Only after a client is moved to visible, heartfelt tears can the therapist and client move forward. Only then can the therapist lift the client's veil and break through the exterior persona. Only then will the client's feelings of loneliness and isolation begin to diminish.

Moses's tears drew Bitya to him, but she was also attracted by something else that was special about this baby. As the Bible tells us, Moses's own mother had described him as "good."

Now I can understand many words used to describe a baby. He looks cute, he looks happy, he looks like his mommy or his daddy. But what does it mean to describe a newborn as "good"?

I understand this "good" as the same "good" that we find in the first verses of Genesis, where the creation of the world is described: "And God said: 'Let there be light.' And there was light. And God saw the light, that it was good."

The light that God created on the first day is difficult to understand. Since the sun, moon, and stars were not created until the fourth day, this light could not have been from one of those heavenly bodies. This light was a Divine life force, an energy, a radiance.

Thus, the description of Moses as "good" represents a new genesis. This is the time for another beginning, for new life, for a radiant life force, for positive energy.

We are not the only creatures instinctively drawn to people or creatures and things that seem to radiate light. My son Isaac recently made me aware of this natural physical phenomenon as he prepared a school science project on phototropism, the phenomenon of plants bending toward a source of light.

We all have the opportunity to bring out our own Divinely given light and to use it as a source of inspiration for ourselves and for others. We can learn to recognize the light and the good in each other, despite our different backgrounds, ethnicities, and beliefs.

The birth of Moses represented a new genesis for the entire world. When Moses's mother first perceived this special light around her child, she remembered the story of creation and saw that this light was good. And the Divine light that surrounded baby Moses stayed with him throughout his life.

Bitya's heartfelt reaction to baby Moses serves as our guide to Moses's ultimate message. He was chosen as the vehicle to teach us that the task of each and every one of us is to bring our light— our Divine life force—to the world.

Moses's birth mother and his adoptive mother came from two different worlds. But the common bond of love and compassion that he absorbed from both of them helped prepare him for the challenges ahead.

CHAPTER 3

A Clash of Cultures

Moses's introduction to the dichotomy of cultures began early in his life. After his birth mother had weaned him, she brought him back to the pharaoh's palace and turned him over to his adoptive mother—the princess.

What happened to him next is a mystery. The Bible doesn't provide many details. First we read about Bitya finding the infant Moses and naming him. Then, the very next verse tells us, "And it came to pass in those days, when Moses was grown up, that he went out unto his brethren, and looked on their burdens."

So where did Moses's childhood go? How did he achieve the values and ethics that later earned him the unique titles of "Servant of God" and "Master of All Prophets"? The very absence of detail forces us to take a very close look at the scant information we do have.

Moses was a young adult—somewhere around twenty—when he "went out unto his brethren," venturing forth beyond the comfortable confines of palace life. Prior to that, he had been pampered and isolated with the other princes and princesses—his stepbrothers and stepsisters—even though he knew he was an Israelite.

Moses was such a favorite of the pharaoh that the pharaoh appointed him as overseer of his entire household. His success echoed that of Joseph, who quickly rose from slavery to a position of trust and power in his master's household.

We can assume that in the pharaoh's court Moses was exposed day and night to a litany of complaints about the enslaved Israelites. He heard that they were no good, they were different, they were not the same race as the Egyptians—probably not even really human—and their lives were cheap and expendable.

Moses's normal, natural reaction would have been to identify totally with his adoptive family rather than his family of origin. An ordinary person would have experienced at least some self-hatred about his "foreign" roots, choosing to identify solely and completely with the privileged, superior people who had taken him in.

But Moses was no ordinary man. The first thing we learn about Moses when he reached mature understanding—"when Moses was grown up"—is that "he went out unto his brethren, and looked on their burdens." Moses got involved!

Moses had nothing to gain and everything to lose by getting involved with the slaves and their problems. He could have felt the way most of us do when we encounter a homeless person lying on a bus bench or a curb or loitering in a doorway. If we look such a person in the eye and discern his or her humanity, we also see parts of ourselves. We are forced to identify with another's predicament and become aware of the fact that we too can become homeless and outcast. It is so much easier to thrust some coins into a person's hand, making sure to avoid any eye contact, or to walk by, pretending not to see.

IDENTIFYING WITH THE OPPRESSED

How easy and how justifiable it would have been for Moses to look the other way. That is how many of us go about our daily lives.

We maintain that we are too busy earning a living or raising a family to get involved in tackling some of today's sticky social issues, even though we know we should be more caring and giving.

But as soon as he reached maturity, Moses "went out"—leaving his comfortable position at the summit of Egyptian life—to learn for himself the nature of the society around him. He immediately witnessed something very troubling: "And he saw an Egyptian man striking a Hebrew man, one of his brethren." Despite Moses's Egyptian upbringing, education, and social conditioning, he was not without compassion. Witnessing the beating of a slave, he cried. He identified with the oppressed, not with the oppressor! Perhaps this moment echoes the time when Bitya, the pharaoh's daughter, cried when she saw the helpless Hebrew infant in the river. No matter what she had been taught, and disregarding the decree of her father, she acted in a way that would save a baby, and ultimately, a people.

When Moses realized that the slave being beaten was indeed suffering, and was indeed human, and was indeed a fellow Hebrew, he took steps that would forever sever him from his comfortable, princely life, and make him a fugitive and an outcast.

"And [Moses] looked this way and that way, and when he saw that there was no man . . ."

"He saw that there was no man." We can take that statement at face value. Moses was prudent. He made sure the coast was clear before he intervened. But here again, the Bible uses that mysterious word for "man," *ish*, which usually refers to a Divine messenger, to someone sent to fulfill a holy mission. Moses may have looked for signs of such a person. Perhaps a stranger would appear, seemingly out of nowhere to take responsibility for this situation.

But there was no one else to intercede—no human or angelic messenger. There was no *ish*. At this moment, Moses realized that the fate of this one suffering Hebrew was in his hands. He had to take personal action and responsibility rather than wait for some miracle to occur. What he did next is difficult to understand.

"He [Moses] killed the Egyptian, and hid him in the sand."

I can understand the need for Moses to intervene and to act decisively. But did he have to *kill* the Egyptian? Might not another, less violent course of action have also been effective? Couldn't a prince of Egypt have ordered the abusive taskmaster to stop beating the slave?

As a psychologist, I am acutely aware of the power of the unconscious—the forces that drive us without our being aware of them. I have also come to understand that the only truths we really possess are what we discover through our actual experiences in life.

Yet, I try to imagine the kind of life that Moses had led up to this point. I think of the traditions that he had inherited. On the one hand, his ancestor Abraham had been known far and wide for his acts of loving-kindness, particularly in welcoming strangers to his tent and to his table. On the other hand, the culture in the pharaoh's palace had taught Moses to fear and revile strangers and foreigners, and to see them as lesser humans.

Another of Moses's Hebrew ancestors, Joseph, had been a tremendous leader who saved the Egyptians from famine. Yet Moses's Egyptian relatives had no problem beating their Hebrew slaves and practically starving them.

Even though Moses had consciously chosen to identify himself as a Hebrew, the darkness that he had absorbed had to surface at some time in his life. We cannot completely separate ourselves from our environment, even when we intentionally distance ourselves from it.

THE CURSE OF INGRATITUDE

In Moses's time, justice was swiftly and brutally administered. The underlying principle was to rely on violent behavior to protect yourself, or better yet, to lash out at potential enemies before they could strike you.

Shortly after Moses slew the Egyptian taskmaster, he went out and "found two Hebrews fighting, so he said to the offender: 'Why do you strike your fellow?' And [the Hebrew] said: 'Who made you a ruler and a judge over us? Do you think to kill me, as you killed the Egyptian?' And Moses was frightened and thought: 'Then the matter is known!'"

This episode is troubling. Moses had looked around very carefully before he struck the Egyptian. No one else was there. Who, then, could have witnessed the attack?

Sherlock Holmes once uttered this astute observation: "When you have eliminated the impossible, whatever remains, however improbable, must be the truth."

Since there were no other witnesses to Moses's act, the only person who could have informed on him was the very person he saved—the Hebrew slave.

It should not surprise us to learn that those we help sometimes turn on us. When we help someone at a time when they are most vulnerable, needy, or embarrassed, they are at first enormously grateful. But then circumstances change. Egypt, for instance, was once needy, and Joseph came to its aid. But when Egypt was no longer needy, the pharaoh chose not to remember Joseph's help, and he turned against Joseph's people.

The Israelite who had been saved by Moses spread the news of Moses's violent deed until it reached the pharaoh. Incensed by the news, the pharaoh ordered that Moses be put to death.

When Moses intervened in the fight between the two Hebrews, he must have been shocked to discover that his secret was public knowledge. He must have been even more shocked by the attitude of one of the Hebrew combatants: "Who made you a ruler and a judge over us?"

Who do you think you are, Moses? You might be the adopted son of the pharaoh, but we all know that you're really Yocheved's son. You're a Hebrew, just like us!

Moses was a Hebrew, yet an Egyptian; a commoner, yet a

member of the royal palace. He had inherited traditions of compassion and caring, as well as those of subjugation and violence. He had intervened in two violent encounters—one between an Egyptian and a Hebrew, and one between two Hebrews. Whatever his own internal conflicts, Moses had developed a universal perspective that let him be compassionate toward the oppressed, no matter who was harming them.

Moses was not naive. He knew that he had to flee to neighboring Midian. This journey would take him to yet another foreign culture, to more encounters with injustice, and to the woman he would marry.

CHAPTER 4

Soul Mates

MOSES'S ESCAPE FROM EGYPT echoed the journeys of a number of his ancestors. Jacob had been forced to flee from the murderous wrath of his brother Esau. Abraham had left his homeland and distanced himself from the idolatrous religion of his father, as he embarked on a mission to forge a new life and a new people in a strange land.

Moses took flight to save his life from the avenging Egyptians. But his journey to Midian had unforeseen outcomes. For one thing, it took him almost immediately into the next phase of his life, into marriage and a family of his own.

In the Bible, the stories about Moses's departure from Egypt and his arrival in Midian are so closely juxtaposed that in the same verse, we read "Moses fled from the face of the pharaoh, and dwelt in the land of Midian; and he sat down by a well."

The brevity and succinctness of this text make it clear that the Moses who championed the underdog and fought against oppression in Egypt was the same Moses who arrived in Midian. Nothing about him had changed during his journey.

Not only that, but the first place that Moses came to was a well. This was yet another illustration of the role of water in his life. As an infant, he had been marked for death by drowning, yet the river had saved him; because of this, he had been named Moses to commemorate being drawn from the water. Perhaps he was instinctively drawn to a well as his first stop in Midian. At that well, we immediately see further proof of Moses's compassionate nature and courage. Just as he arrived at the well, he witnessed an ugly, violent incident.

The Bible describes the scene with just a few words, but the picture painted by the Midrash is clear enough. The priest of Midian, Jethro, has seven daughters, who have come to water their father's flock. But they are surrounded by shepherds who harass and assault them. The defenseless young women are at the mercy of these men, who try to rape them.

Some questions immediately occur to readers of this text. Who is Jethro, this priest of Midian? If he is such a high-ranking member of Midianite society, why are his daughters forced to do such menial labor by themselves? And why do the shepherds harass them?

Jethro is one of the most interesting characters in the Bible. The Midrash fills in some of the details about his life. For many years, he was known and respected throughout Midian as the high priest of its idolatrous religion, and he was treated like royalty.

But then, something pivotal happened in Jethro's life. At some point, he began to question the belief system that he inherited from his ancestors. He started to wonder how idols that were fashioned and molded by human beings could possess Divine powers. As his doubts mounted, he slowly turned away from idol worship to another faith that made more sense to him.

FINDING TRUTHS FOR OURSELVES

Jethro's change of heart came about only partly because of his own intellectual exploration, the Midrash says. The truths that we discover and internalize are not based solely on intellectual development. They stem also from our own personal encounters and experiences in life.

After Jethro had begun to perceive the world differently than his countrymen, he heard about the pharaoh's harsh decrees concerning the enslavement and attempted annihilation of the Israelites. How could it be, he wondered, that one people should enslave another just because they were different? How could the Egyptians forget so quickly how Joseph—a Hebrew—had saved their entire country from famine? How could they repay good with evil? Didn't their behavior demonstrate that idolatry, such as that practiced in Egypt and Midian, was morally and ethically bankrupt?

Jethro was fundamentally ethical, and his social status gave him the self-confidence and the courage to act boldly, to break with his past and the culture that surrounded him. He gradually came to believe in ethical monotheism, and he converted his entire family to his new faith. The Midrash tells us that when Jethro severed his ties with idolatry, he was forced to relinquish his power and position, and he and his family became outcasts, scorned by their fellow Midianites.

All this explains why Jethro's daughters were tending their sheep by themselves. When their family had wealth and power, this task would have been delegated to someone else.

As the shepherds began advancing to rape the young women, Moses came to their rescue, chasing off the attackers and staying to help the women water their flock.

Once again, Moses had chosen to get involved, even though he had just arrived in Midian. He dealt swiftly and decisively with injustice, just as he had in Egypt. And he was soon rewarded for his noble actions.

When Jethro's daughters returned home, their father asked how they had managed to water their flocks so quickly. They responded with the story of Moses's courageous rescue, and Jethro, who appreciated good deeds, promptly invited this stranger to his home. After a time, Jethro offered Moses a bride—his beautiful, kind daughter Zipporah, who had been as zealous as her father in embracing the new religion.

SEEKING THE LIGHT OF COMPANIONSHIP

We might at first think of Zipporah as an unlikely spouse for Moses. After all, she was a convert to his faith, and had a very different cultural background. Of course, many of us think that love is guided by the laws of magnetism. To some extent that may be true, since people with opposite traits often complement each other. But there is a deeper form of attraction, one based on shared experiences and values. That type of longing represents the yearning of the soul for a true soul mate. If the search is successful, such a match will enable each partner to feel understood, nurtured, and happy.

Moses and Zipporah had much more in common than we usually realize. Like Moses, Zipporah evolved from a blend of two cultures—her native Midianite society and her adopted Hebrew identity. Like Moses, she was reared as a child of the royal class, but now experienced life as a commoner. Like Moses, she had been hurt by people who were supposed to be her friends. She knew what it was like to suffer, and her ethical character ensured that she would put that experience to good use and spend her life trying to help others. Furthermore, she would understand, appreciate, and support Moses's central task in life: fighting on behalf of the oppressed. She would share not only his values, but also his mission. When Moses would return home after labors, Zipporah would greet him warmly and be there to appreciate what he told her about his day. They would function together as a mutually supportive team.

The Austrian poet Rainer Maria Rilke, wondering if such an understanding relationship is possible, wrote in *Duino Elegies:*

"Who, if I cried out, would hear me then, out of the orders of angels?" Zipporah would be Moses's angel. Even though Moses and Zipporah would share an earthly partnership, it would be guided by the loftiest spiritual values and goals.

I envisioned their relationship in a new light after visiting the home of a friend—a bright, sensitive, insightful young woman, with many hobbies and interests, including art. As I walked into her living room, I was immediately struck by two similar—yet different—copies of Chagall paintings hanging on opposite walls. One was called "On the Promenade," and the other was "Over the Town." There were identical male and female images in both pictures. However, in "On the Promenade," the man stood on the ground, with his arms extended upwards. The woman was flying above him, reaching down and taking his hands in hers. By contrast, in "Over the Town," the figures were intertwined as they flew through space together.

As he went forth to help the oppressed, Moses would need someone to fly with him. In Zipporah, he found his spiritual mate. They married, and Zipporah soon gave birth to a son, whom Moses named Gershom, which was derived from the Hebrew words *ger* ("stranger") and *shom* ("there"). Moses explained this choice of a name by saying, "I have been a stranger in a strange land."

Moses continued to dwell in Midian, working as a shepherd and tending the flock of his father-in-law Jethro, and taking great care in looking after the sheep, especially the young lambs who would wander away from the flock.

God observed the kindness of Moses, the shepherd who cared for all the sheep, as well as his other fine character traits. No wonder God would soon appear to Moses from the midst of a burning bush, calling on him to become the shepherd of Israel.

CHAPTER 5

The Burning Bush

CERTAIN QUALITIES that Moses demonstrated as a shepherd caused God to select him as the future shepherd of a people. His actions indicated what sort of man he really was.

For example, the Midrash describes Moses's meticulous concern for the safety and welfare of each animal. Since the value of the flock is always the primary concern of any shepherd, we might think that only the animals of greatest worth—that is, the strongest adult sheep—got Moses's attention. After all, if a small or malnourished or weak lamb wandered off, wouldn't that just be a part of the process of natural selection? Only the best and hardiest of the animals would survive.

But Moses was not that type of shepherd. The Midrash describes how one day, while Moses was feeding Jethro's flock, he saw a little lamb wandering away from the others. He quickly followed it and succeeded in overtaking it at a brook where the lamb had stopped to quench its thirst. Moses stooped to pick it up and apologized: "If I had known you were thirsty, I would have taken you in my arms and carried you here myself." At that moment, a Heavenly Voice called out: "By your life, Moses, you are fit to shepherd Israel."

God recognized that Moses cared for all the sheep, and that he would care for all the people, even those who might spiritually wander off from the fold.

One day, as he and his flock were out in the wilderness, Moses had an extraordinary spiritual experience. "And the angel of the Lord appeared unto him in a flame of fire out of the midst of a bush; and he looked, and, behold, the bush burned with fire, and the bush was not consumed."

Notice that the verse says the angel of the Lord appeared "unto him." So we recognize that although other shepherds were with him, only Moses was privy to this mystical vision. And what an unusual vision it was.

It was a thorn bush, a wild acacia, which is very common in that region. But Moses knew that this was no ordinary shrub. Just as he had concerned himself with the plight of the smallest, lowliest lamb, so too did he interest himself in the lowliest bush. He took the time and effort to go out of his way to investigate why it was burning. Once again, he demonstrated his readiness to get involved. And God, now even more certain of Moses's outstanding character, spoke to him, calling, as the Bible says, "out of the midst of the bush: 'Moses, Moses.' And he said: 'Here I am.'"

The Hebrew word for the bush that Moses saw is *sneh*. If you say it out loud, you will recognize that it is related to another famous word in the Bible—Sinai, as in Mount Sinai, where Moses would later receive the Ten Commandments. Why should the name of this small plant resemble that of the mountain? One lesson to be learned from the use of these words is that just as God can appear at the summit of a mountain, God can also make the Divine Presence known at the lowliest bush in the wilderness. God is everywhere and with everyone, protecting the mighty, the humble, the frail, and the vulnerable.

We can learn other lessons from the story of Moses and the burning bush. For example, notice how Moses responded when God called to him from out of the bush. He answered, "Here I am."

"Here I am" is more than just a "present and accounted for." It suggests, "I'm ready to undertake whatever you ask of me."

When most people are called upon to perform a task or fulfill some higher calling, they tend to answer, "Sorry, I'm too busy right now. Maybe next week." Or, we might expect that Moses would have replied, "Sorry, I've had a long and tiring day out here with the sheep. Maybe another time." But Moses demonstrated once again that he was ready to become involved.

HOW MOSES OVERCAME HIS DOUBTS

The bush that Moses saw was engulfed in flame, yet it was *not consumed*. The bush symbolizes for all times and for all people that good eventually triumphs over evil. In the course of our often difficult lives, we ask ourselves which forces will ultimately triumph over others. But the bush tells us that there will always be some destructive elements in our lives—like the fire. However, the good elements—like the bush—will endure and not be consumed.

As Moses stood before the burning bush, God told him to "remove your shoes from your feet, for the place on which you stand is holy ground."

Why must Moses take off his shoes?

Shoes protect us from the harshness of the ground, and Moses was being told to divest himself of anything that might be a barrier between himself and the ground upon which he walked. He was to feel the earth beneath him, the pebbles and grains of sand under his feet. This sensitivity would be necessary for him to lead, since a leader's sensitivity must be fine-tuned to the feelings of the people.

God began to explain Moses's mission. We learn that God had been moved by the cries of the Israelites who were being afflicted by their cruel Egyptian taskmasters. God told Moses that the God of Moses's forefathers would deliver the Israelites to the Promised Land, a place flowing with milk and honey. But first, Moses had to intervene with the pharaoh on behalf of the Israelites and then lead them on their journey to freedom.

We might expect that after having witnessed such an extra-ordinary vision as the burning bush and then hearing God's voice, Moses would be filled with tremendous awe and reverence. *Of course*, he would want to be part of God's plan. After all, he had initially responded, "Here I am."

But Moses—the great leader-to-be—did not jump into action. Of God, Moses had one basic question, one which demonstrated his humility and his feelings of inadequacy: "Who am I, that I should go unto pharaoh?"

Like any human being, Moses knew himself better than any-one else. He may have been aware of his royal upbringing, but he was also cognizant of what he regarded as his inadequacies and inferior qualities. So God responded to Moses in a way that not only gave Moses strength, but also has continued to provide strength and guidance to each of us throughout the generations. God said, "I will be with you."

In addition to realizing that he would never be alone, Moses learned from God that he would return with the Israelites to this sacred spot. But then, he would not stand before the lowly bush—the *sneh*—where he now found himself. He would be atop the ad-jacent Mount *Sinai*, receiving the tablets of the Law. And those teachings would represent the core of the entire mission of Moses and of the people he would lead. That Torah would be the blue-print for ideal human behavior, and teach humanity that our task is to fight oppression, ensure justice, and protect the defenseless.

Moses's life was dedicated to these goals. But he was more than a great leader. He was the master of all prophets. His prophetic visions and encounters were unique, and he was aware of his special relationship with God. Now he dared to ask God another question: "What should I tell the Israelites is Your Name?"

God responded that the Name of the Divinity is *Ehyeh*, meaning "I will always be with you." Just as God had previously assured Moses that "I will be with you," God now informed Moses that this quality was actually God's Eternal Name! He wanted the Israelites to understand that even in their suffering, their God was present and would be there to lead them to redemption.

This was a profound and powerful message. Just as Moses would not be alone, we will never be alone. An anonymous story entitled "Footprints" beautifully illustrates this truth.

> One night a man had a dream. He dreamed he was walking along the beach with the Lord. Across the sky flashed scenes from his life. For each scene, he noticed two sets of footprints in the sand: one belonging to him, and the other to the Lord.
>
> When the last scene of his life flashed before him, he looked back at the footprints in the sand. He noticed that many times along the path of his life there was only one set of footprints. He also noticed that it happened at the very lowest and saddest times in his life.
>
> This really bothered him and he questioned the Lord about it. "Lord, you said that once I decided to follow You, You'd walk with me all the way. But I have noticed that during the most troublesome times in my life, there is only one set of footprints. I don't understand why, when I needed you most, You would leave me."
>
> The Lord replied, "My precious, precious child, I love you and I would never leave you. During your times of trial and suffering, when you see only one set of footprints, it was then that I carried you."

Most of us go through life experiencing intermittent feelings of loneliness. This is true whether or not we are married, or are parents, or have children or brothers or sisters, or even close friends. There are times when, confronted with suffering or with existential concerns, we feel very alone indeed. But God's response to Moses teaches us again that we are never completely alone, and that God will always be with us.

Even while knowing all this, Moses was still not ready to take on the mission. He anticipated that his fellow Israelites would give him trouble. After all, even though he had personally experienced the Divine, they had not. They would have to be convinced of the Divine promise—as well as of Moses's role in it—before they would follow him out of the land of Egypt.

CHAPTER 6

Doubt

Moses's reaction to the divine call was—to put it mildly—puzzling, considering that God had appeared to him, promising to redeem the Israelites from their bondage and to always be with Moses. God had also assured Moses that the people would listen to the story of his Divine encounter at the burning bush. But despite these assurances, Moses seemed unconvinced that he was up to the task.

We might think that, filled with fervor and enthusiasm, Moses would respond to his Divine call with a loud "Amen." After all, that is the usual response to a heartfelt prayer or even to a rousing sermon. Moses had even heard the Divine Voice!

When we respond "Amen," we are making an affirmation. It is an abbreviated way of saying, "I confirm that God is trustworthy. I agree with that."

But instead of answering "Amen," Moses replied that the people "will *not* answer 'Amen' to what I tell them." What can this mean?

When we are completely convinced of something in our own hearts, we have no doubts about it. In our certainty, we also feel confident that we can persuade others about what we believe.

Perhaps Moses's response to God conveyed something very subtle about his own state of mind at that moment. Perhaps his concern about the people's possible reaction actually reflected *his own* doubts.

After all, Moses was surely mindful of the vindictive ruler of Egypt from whom he had fled for his life. He also remembered that the pharaoh's court included mighty magicians who regularly exhibited their wonders. How would he measure up when they demonstrated their power? Additionally, Moses wondered how the enslaved Hebrews would be able to believe or even listen to his tales of a burning bush while they were being whipped by their oppressors. The people might dismiss him or denounce him as crazy.

Moses also recognized that the Israelites constituted a huge group of two or three million people. They would need food and shelter, as well as astute leadership, to get them through the wilderness to the Promised Land.

So even though Moses may have been 99 percent convinced by God that his mission would be successful, he could not help having a few second thoughts. And it is that 1 percent of doubt—Moses's own inner doubt—that he projected onto the rest of his people.

SPEAKING TRUTH TO POWER

Moses pleaded, "They will not believe me. They will not listen to my voice." God heard and understood. He realized that Moses was concerned about having something tangible to show the people that would supplement his words and his tale about the burning bush. God also knew that Moses would need some concrete signs to match or outdo the pharaoh's magicians. So God provided him with what he needed. "The Lord said unto him: 'What is that in your hand?' And he said: 'A rod.' And He said: 'Cast it on the ground.' And he cast in on the ground, and it became a serpent. . . . And the Lord said unto Moses: 'Put forth your hand, and take it by the tail'—and he put forth his hand, and laid hold of it, and it became a rod in his hand."

In this exchange, God seemed to be saying: "Look, you already have something magical in your possession. You already have the power. Your rod is just an extension of your own arm, your own body. Once you believe in your own abilities, you will be empowered to perform the miracles that I will direct you to carry out."

God proceeded to show Moses more wonders that he could use to convince the Israelites of his Divine mission. God made Moses's hand become leprous, and then returned it to its normal state. God told Moses that as a final sign, he should take water from the Nile and place it upon the dry land, where it would be turned into blood. Thus, Moses would be able to demonstrate God's power to help convince the Israelites to listen to him and believe what he said.

From the effort that God expended to counter Moses's doubts, we learn that God understands that spirituality is difficult for us to maintain if it exists only in the psychic realm. We need some demonstration of it in our physical reality as well. Even something as simple as an angel pin in our lapel can help remind us that we are not alone.

If we cannot achieve this integrated approach to the way we see our lives, there will be consequences. Some of these may be physical. Moses, for example, was a stutterer. He openly expressed his doubts to God about his ability to speak to the Israelites and to the pharaoh: "I am not a man of words . . . for I have heaviness of speech, and heaviness of tongue."

A number of theories exist about the etiology of stuttering. Some say that it starts with an overbearing mother or father who does not give the child adequate opportunity to speak. Others say that it comes from being raised in turbulent, difficult times, or that it stems from the fear of having to talk to an intimidating authority figure who only pays attention to the confident and powerful.

According to the Midrash, this is how Moses became a stutterer:

One day, when he was three years old, he was playing in a room with other members of the pharaoh's household. The pharaoh was seated nearby on his throne. Suddenly, Moses snatched the crown off the pharaoh's head and placed it on his own head. The pharaoh and his advisors were horrified and tried to determine how best to respond. One of the advisors suggested that this had not been a playful accident at all, but rather a willful act by the young Moses, who would grow up to one day destroy Egypt.

A test was quickly devised. A precious gem would be placed on a table, and next to it would be a pan of hot coals. Moses would be set before these two objects. If he reached for the gem, he would demonstrate his desire to usurp the pharaoh's throne, and he would be put to death. If he reached for the coals, he would prove that he was innocent of any wrongdoing and his life would be spared.

Moses was brought into the room. He was immediately attracted to the bright, shiny jewel and started to reach for it. But an angel nudged his hand toward the pan of coals. Moses picked up a hot coal and touched his mouth with it, burning his lips and tongue and causing him to become "heavy of speech and of tongue." So the cause of Moses's stuttering may be truly unique.

FINDING THE PURPOSE OF OUR IMPEDIMENTS

I stuttered when I was a child. Speech therapy helped me gain a greater degree of fluency. But years later, during my own psychological analysis, I learned to integrate my varying beliefs and life experiences and found that my speech improved tremendously. I have concluded that stuttering may well relate to a poor integration of our experiences. We may *know* something intellectually, but if we have not experienced it, we will face cognitive dissonance—many different internal voices, each struggling to be heard.

When Moses complained of his speech impediment, God responded with these rhetorical questions: "Who has made man's mouth? . . . Is it not I the Lord?" Thus, God conveyed the message that we are all fashioned—and empowered—by God. Each one of us has been given the specific tools we need to be a vehicle for *God's Voice*.

On a wall of my office hangs a picture featuring a prayer that expresses my feelings at the beginning of each day. Attributed to Maimonides, the great Jewish physician and philosopher, the prayer reads: "I am ready, preparing myself to be engaged in my healing activities. Please, Almighty God, assist me in my endeavors so that my efforts will succeed." Mindful of my former stutter, I pray for Divine guidance in carrying out my responsibilities and duties, particularly with regard to finding the words that I hope will bring healing, comfort, and understanding to those who seek my counsel.

It is important for each of us to realize that just as God has designed our challenge, God will help us find a way to meet it. The patriarch Jacob was left limping after his encounter with an angel, and he found strength by leaning upon a walking stick. Moses, who was not fluent in his speech, felt that he needed something or someone to lean on. Responding to Moses's concerns, God promised him that his older brother Aaron would be at his side and would articulate what Moses wanted to tell the pharaoh. He would also speak for Moses to the Hebrews.

Moses would begin his mission with a lot of help. He would have the promise of God's presence, a repertoire of wonders to perform, and the assistance of Aaron. Yet, even with all this support, Moses would still face a lonely night journey of the soul. He would experience a crisis of faith.

CHAPTER 7

Crisis of Faith

Moses prepared to set off on his journey, taking in his hand his powerful walking stick, now called "the rod of God." This phrase indicates that Moses felt empowered and was aware of God's constant presence.

He was ready—at last—to fulfill his mission.

But first, he returned to his father-in-law for a blessing for his journey to Egypt. Jethro gave Moses his wholehearted support, telling him to go in peace. Moses would indeed need this blessing along his way. His travels would bring him to a crisis of faith that nearly resulted in his death.

As Moses's journey began, he was accompanied by his wife and his sons. *Sons?* We know about only one son—Gershom. But from this plural form, we learn that Zipporah had just given birth to another son, whose name—we later discover—is Eliezer. Moses was undoubtedly overjoyed to have a second child, yet his happiness was short-lived. Before he and his family could continue on their way, God appeared to him. What Moses heard from God shook his belief system to the core.

God revealed to Moses exactly how the Egyptians would be punished, and Moses could not believe what he heard. First, God would harden the pharaoh's heart, so that he would refuse to let the Israelites go. Second, God told Moses to inform the pharaoh that Israel was God's firstborn "son," and when pharaoh refused to let this "son" go, God would kill all the firstborn sons of the Egyptians, including the pharaoh's.

These harsh decrees were different from anything Moses had ever heard before from God. His confused reaction is hinted at in the opening words of the very next verse: "And it came to pass on the way at the lodging-place." Moses was metaphorically "on the way"—in the middle of his life's journey. We should not be surprised that God's disturbing message propelled him into a midlife crisis of faith.

What Moses experienced is universal. As Dante wrote in *The Inferno*: "Midway in life's journey, I found myself in a dark wood, having lost the way." Moses had lost his direction and sense of purpose. His story is instructive for the rest of us who lose our way from time to time.

Every day, people come to my office in pain, anxious to spill out their deepest fears and doubts. The amazing thing is that each client thinks he or she is the only person experiencing life this way. Somehow, we often assume that, for other people, life is easier. Even more than that, many religious clients seem to believe that it is wrong to have doubts about their beliefs—or at least wrong to express them. But I can point to this story about Moses and demonstrate that even he was bewildered by what he experienced.

FACING THE DARK SIDE OF GOD

Moses's crisis of faith is understandable. How can the God who proposed to harden the pharaoh's heart and kill the firstborn of Egypt be the same God who loved Abraham, Isaac, and Jacob, the same God who created light for the world? Just a short time before this, Moses had been reassured by a benevolent God Who promised to always be by his side. Now God seemed to present a totally different face.

Moses was the father figure and the shepherd of his people, yet even he experienced this crisis of the soul. All of us, at various points in our lives, also face the dark, judgmental, shadow side of God. All of us experience physical illness, sometimes emotional illness, and, of course, death. These are intrinsic, challenging parts of the human condition, and we spend most of our lives trying to figure out the answers to our deepest, most troubling questions. And we are afraid because we recognize that our lifelong dialogue with God is not conducted on an equal footing: we remain in awe of the Divine powers to create and destroy.

As Moses lay under the stars, trying to go to sleep, I imagine he mulled over all that he had been told. Night is when our inner conflicts and personal crises come to the fore. As the great philosopher Friedrich Nietzsche wrote in *Thus Spoke Zarathustra:* "Sleeping is no mean art. . . . Few know it, but one must have all the virtues to sleep well. . . . Peace with God and the neighbor: that is what good sleep demands."

Moses tossed and turned. He did not feel at peace with God, and he wondered how God could decide to harden a man's heart. After all, one of the basic tenets of his faith was the gift of free will. Wouldn't the pharaoh be granted the opportunity to exercise his own free will?

Moses also pondered God's plan to kill the Egyptian firstborn sons. Again, this was not the image of God with which Moses was familiar. It sounded like retribution carried out by a vindictive God. How could innocent children suffer for the sins of their fathers? It appeared that God was condemning people to death just because they were firstborn babies, regardless of their own merits, or those of other family members. The death of the firstborn would include pharaoh's eldest son, who was both *Moses's stepbrother* and Bitya's brother. Bitya had demonstrated her greatness by looking at the baby Moses as an individual, not as part of a hated people. Was *her* heart to be broken by God? I imagine that a bewildered Moses wondered, "Shouldn't each Egyptian have the right to be judged as an individual?"

Moses's questions are very difficult. They have endured throughout the generations. Ancient and modern biblical commentators have tried to address the complex issue of free will. For example, Maimonides understood that God had hardened pharaoh's heart as part of the pharaoh's punishment. The pharaoh's normal capacity to repent was taken away from him because he had so harshly treated the Hebrews. Although I understand what Maimonides is saying, I must admit that I have never found his or any other interpretation of the hardening of the pharaoh's heart wholly convincing. But just this past year, I had an *experience* that let me see this unfathomable episode from a different perspective, allowing me to approach it in a new way.

I was counseling a young couple who had been married for eight years. Their marriage seemed to be deeply troubled. When I first met them, I was impressed with the husband's pleasant, compassionate manner. He said, "I really want to make this marriage succeed. I'm willing to work at it. I'll give therapy ten sessions to see if it can work. I'm willing to change some of my behavior, and if my wife is able to make some changes during the first five sessions, that'll be a great sign that we're on the right track. I'm really hoping for the best."

We began our work together and seemed to cover a lot of ground during a short period of time. The wife began to reassess how she distanced herself from her husband. However, by the eighth session, it became apparent that she was not making any real effort to change her intimate conduct with her husband. What struck me most was the dramatic change in the husband's behavior during that meeting. Even though two more sessions remained, he no longer believed his wife would change. He had hardened his heart. He was angry and loud, and behaved that way during the rest of the sessions. At our tenth meeting, he shouted at his wife, "I said I'd give it ten sessions, and now it's clear that you won't change. I want a divorce!"

Later that night, after I had time to digest what had happened and reflect upon the husband's reaction, I gained new insight into the meaning of God's hardening the pharaoh's heart. The biblical text makes it clear that for many of the initial plagues, the pharaoh had complete free will. Each time that the Egyptians were afflicted—with blood, frogs, lice, wild animals, and pestilence—the pharaoh promised to change his ways. But after the plagues were rescinded, he went back on his word. Therefore, for the later plagues, God hardened the pharaoh's heart.

God truly wanted the pharaoh to repent and change his ways and let the Israelites go. If he had done so, he and his people would have been spared any further misfortune. However, the pharaoh demonstrated that he could not be transformed. Therefore, he was given no more chances. By his lack of sincere repentance and effort to change, he needed to be shown that the awesome power responsible for the plagues could be used even against the innocent. By the time of the tenth plague, God and the pharaoh were ready for the ultimate punishment—the killing of the firstborn.

But Moses still found it terribly difficult to accept such a harsh decree. I imagine that he could not understand the threat to his own Egyptian family, to those very people who had saved his life. Furthermore, he had just become a father again, and he had a heightened awareness of the bond between a father and his child. This made him bewildered as he thought of such a loving bond being severed. It seemed to Moses as if his God, by threatening to destroy children, was somehow acting in the same manner as the pharaoh, and that did not sit right with him.

CONFRONTING OUR ULTIMATE SOLITUDE

Moses's inner struggle was about the nature of good and evil. Life is a constant struggle between these two forces, and the greatest works of literature reflect this universal theme. We face our lives with the knowledge that the way will be difficult, and that our journey will be lonely. In Jens Peter Jacobsen's classic Danish novel, *Niels Lyhne,* the title character explores his feelings on his deathbed, reflecting on this central tragedy of life: "It was the great sadness that a soul is always alone."

It is not surprising that even Moses is puzzled by the human condition and by life's mysteries. What is astonishing, however, is that he responds in a way that seems out of character and almost inconceivable.

Moses decides that he will *not* perform a ritual circumcision on his newborn son, which is customarily performed on the eighth day after birth. He will not enter him into the covenant of Abraham, the sacred cornerstone of Israelite tradition and identity.

Moses defies the covenant with God! Can you imagine such defiance? Every time I read this story, I think of my own role as the spiritual leader of a large congregation. Each Yom Kippur, I conduct services at Cedars-Sinai Medical Center in Los Angeles for about a thousand people. Suppose my newborn son were due to be circumcised that day, but instead of performing that ritual, I stood up in front of the entire congregation and said: "Ladies and gentlemen, I am truly sorry, but I cannot go on with the circumcision as planned. Yesterday, I visited with a family that has just lost an infant daughter. They are wonderful people, and they really wanted this child after nine years of trying to conceive. As I cried with them, I felt confused, shaken, and alone. I am having religious doubts. Therefore, I cannot proceed as scheduled."

I can imagine what the reaction might be. People would be upset and angry. Some might yell: "What do you think you're doing? What kind of rabbi are you? Why don't you let someone else take over the services?" Even if some people can admit their own religious doubts, they usually do not allow their leaders to express doubts.

Leaders are usually held to higher standards than followers. Moses would be held to the highest standards of all, since he was the greatest leader of all. Perhaps he felt he was still free to act on his doubts. After all, he was not yet responsible to his followers. But he certainly was accountable to God, to Whom he had already promised he would carry out his assigned mission. When his refusal to circumcise Eliezer belied that promise, God's response was immediate and angry. In yet another illustration of Divine power, God let Moses know that his life was at stake. Moses still had a chance to make the right decision and save himself, but God let him know that the mission to Egypt would be carried out with or without his involvement.

This is when Moses had a near-death experience. According to the Midrash, Moses suddenly found himself totally incapacitated, lying on the ground. Different ailments began to attack various parts of his body—some working their way from his head downward, some rising up from the soles of his feet. He grew weaker and thought he would probably die momentarily. Suddenly, all the illnesses converged at the site of his genitals, pointing to the cause of Moses's sickness, namely, not circumcising his son.

Moses's wife, Zipporah, who had been watching in horror, suddenly realized exactly what she had to do to save her husband's life.

CHAPTER 8

A New View

ZIPPORAH ACTED QUICKLY and decisively to save Moses. When she realized that his suffering was related to not circumcising their new son, Zipporah quickly grabbed a sharp stone and used it to remove Eliezer's foreskin, circumcising him in accordance with God's covenant. Just as suddenly, Moses's illness disappeared, and he quickly recovered. This highly significant episode teaches us many lessons, even as it raises more questions. For example, how could Zipporah carry out the circumcision? In the surrounding cultures and among the Israelites, only men performed this important rite. Even today, among traditional Jews, circumcisions are performed by males. How could Zipporah have dared to undertake such a task? She could easily have thought, "I can't do that. That's a man's role!"

But, as we have seen from the circumstances surrounding this event, she really felt that she had no choice. She had to rise to the occasion. There is a saying in *Pirke Avot, The Ethics of the Fathers,* a volume of rabbinic wisdom: "In a place where there are no people, strive to be a person."

Certainly, when there is no one else around who can carry out a vital mission, you have to take risks and attempt things that you otherwise would not do. Such was the case with Zipporah, who found herself in the middle of the desert with a disabled husband and no one else to help her. Moreover, even if there *is* someone else around, but that person does not have the courage to do the right thing, you must stand up and be counted.

I recall a patient whom I visited in my hospital's cardiology unit about three years ago.

"Rabbi," he said, "I'm a hard-driving, highly successful guy, and I've always prided myself on my good health. When I get a cold, I always take a decongestant to clear things up right away, and no one ever sees me with a runny nose. The other day, my wife and I were strolling through Beverly Hills, and I felt some shortness of breath. But it didn't seem to be anything to worry about. And then, the night before last, I broke out in a sweat and felt some chest pains."

At this point, his wife spoke up. "I begged him to pay attention to these signs, but he's so stubborn, rabbi. Totally in denial. Finally, I got up, got dressed, and told him that I was taking him to the emergency room at Cedars-Sinai. At first, he wouldn't listen to me, but I insisted. I never thought I could be so assertive.

"To make a long story short, the doctors ran some tests and discovered that his left coronary artery was 95 percent blocked. They did an angioplasty and opened it up. The resident in charge said to me, 'Lady, if you hadn't brought him in when you did, he'd be dead.'"

That woman rose to the occasion, even when her actions were contrary to the way she had consistently behaved throughout twenty years of marriage. Many other women are similarly called upon to deal decisively with life-and-death emergencies.

A woman gynecologist gave me some insight into the source of such female resilience. She explained that women are not usually as squeamish about blood as men. During her childbearing years, a woman generally experiences her menstrual cycle every month and is attuned to the rhythm of these changes within her body. Every time that she sees her menstrual blood, she is aware, at least on an unconscious level, that a potential life has not come to be—a kind of death has taken place. At the same time, the show of blood indicates that the woman still has the ability to be a mother, should she want to be, and that there is always the hope for a new life to be created in the months ahead.

THE POWER OF OUR UNIQUE PERSPECTIVE

Not only was Zipporah a woman, but she was also a convert to her husband's faith. Her unique perspective gave her the strength to act when needed. Born into a pagan society that worshiped idols, Zipporah was familiar with deities that were fearsome and demanding. One idol in particular, Molech, was appeased only by child sacrifices. So hearing that the firstborn of the Egyptians would be slain, the Midrash tells us Zipporah was not so shocked. She also understood that these children would not die to *appease* any deity. On the contrary, as awful as the loss of the firstborn would be, it would be part of the process of redeeming an en-slaved people.

Zipporah could embrace this concept. When she heard of God's plan to kill the Egyptian firstborn, she did not react as Moses did. Zipporah had a different way of understanding events, a world perspective that Moses did not yet grasp.

Even if Zipporah had not come from a culture like Midian's, being a convert made her central to this story. I am sure that many of you have heard about someone converting to another faith and becoming more devout than most of the people who were born into that religion. To convert is to be spiritually reborn. As a matter of fact, part of the Jewish conversion ritual involves immersion in a body of water, which is a symbolic womb. When the convert emerges from the water, he or she experiences a form of rebirth. Thus, conversion is the quintessential statement of hope and optimism. The convert has experienced a new beginning, a new life, and knows that change and growth are always possible.

Such sentiments have often been shared with me by a dear friend Rebecca, who converted to Judaism some three years ago. She has always had a rather sunny disposition, but since her conversion, she describes herself as "rejuvenated," "joyful," and "optimistic." Not surprisingly, she continues to help her husband, who was born to the faith, with his spiritual growth and development. Another friend and convert, Melinda, has become a teacher of others. While sharing her considerable knowledge, she also serves as a role model of exemplary behavior. She continues to find happiness in her new faith as she enriches the spirituality of those around her.

Zipporah teaches us a lot about the role of women and of converts. She also illustrates the pivotal role of a spouse. Life is too hard to go through alone, and we sometimes rely on our spouse to help us do the right thing. Zipporah taught this to Moses when she acted so decisively.

Zipporah's tremendous enthusiasm for the values she had adopted, her optimism about the future, and her role as a supportive wife helped her during this critical event. Even when she saw that her husband was near death, she did not lose hope and was confident that her actions could make a difference.

It is frightening to think what might have happened had Zipporah not acted. Moses might have died, and the entire history of the Israelites might have unfolded in a completely different way.

Zipporah's act is instructive in yet another way. She reached for a flint (*tzor* in Hebrew) to perform the circumcision on her son. That word teaches us a lot. It is related to a very similar word, *tzar*, which means "narrow," just as the flint is narrow. This term often has negative connotations. For example, the Hebrew name for Egypt is *Mitzrayim*, which suggests that Egypt represented a narrow, dangerous place for the Israelites.

From the similarity of the words for "flint" and for "a narrow place," we learn something very important. Our actions are central. A sharp stone may be a tool—or a weapon. What we do has the power to hurt others—or to bring about redemption. The choice is ours.

Zipporah chose well. After she circumcised Eliezer, Moses recovered. It is as if Moses's level of faith had been monitored on an EEG machine. Profound distress might create strong waves, rapidly moving up and down, causing the recording device to shake vigorously. But at the end of the test, the patient is still alive and well. Only when the EEG is completely flat is there no hope, only then is the patient dead.

Moses was alive, but still weak. God sent Moses's brother Aaron to help him and accompany him on the rest of his journey to Egypt. When the brothers met in the desert, Moses conveyed to Aaron all that God had told him about their mission.

The brothers arrived in Egypt and demonstrated to the Israelites the wonders that God had empowered them to perform. When the people saw these signs, they believed they would be redeemed, and responded, "Amen." With the support of his family and his people, Moses finally found the inner strength to go forward.

PART II

The Miraculous Deliverance

CHAPTER 9

The First Intervention

M OSES AND AARON FINALLY ARRIVED at the pharaoh's court, faced with a difficult and complex mission: to persuade the pharaoh to free the enslaved Israelites. They needed to choose their words carefully. Even more important than what they would say would be how they said it. To resolve differences of opinion, both sides must communicate effectively, yet it was clear that a huge gap existed between the pharaoh and Moses and Aaron. They viewed the world from very different perspectives, so unless Moses and Aaron made themselves very clear, true dialogue between the two sides would be impossible.

They began by telling the pharaoh: "Thus says the Lord, the God of Israel: Let My people go, that they may hold a feast unto Me in the wilderness." All they were asking for at this point was a three-day holiday for the Israelites, but it was quite evident, right from the outset, that no communication was taking place. The pharaoh had never heard of this God of Israel. He felt quite bewildered.

The pharaoh saw the world from his rather narrow point of view. He was not only an absolute ruler with complete power over his subjects, but also, according to the Midrash, he considered himself a god. He even thought that he had created the river Nile! So how could he believe that another power was superior to himself? Moreover, this pharaoh could only understand physical realities—himself, his idols, his pyramids, his cities. He could not relate to the invisible God whom Moses and Aaron described.

The pharaoh made his lack of understanding abundantly clear. He immediately asked: "Who is the Lord, that I should hearken unto His voice to let Israel go?" It was not surprising that he would respond this way. He was certain that he knew about every other power in the universe, and he had not heard about this God. The Midrash explains that the pharaoh had looked through all the scrolls in his library, reading about the gods of neighboring nations, without finding any reference to the God of Israel, the Creator of the universe. After completing this search, he angrily said to Moses and Aaron, "I know not the Lord, and moreover I will not let Israel go." So it was up to Moses and Aaron to teach the pharaoh something essential about God.

When the pharaoh said that he did not "know" God, he meant that he had not personally experienced God. Moses, by contrast, had stood before the burning bush and experienced a vision of the Lord that other shepherds nearby didn't see. Moses came to realize that there are two kinds of realities: the inner reality of the unconscious and the external reality of the physical. But he could not describe what it was like to actually experience the Divine. He knew firsthand about *Ehyeh,* the all-powerful, everpresent, compassionate, caring God, but there was no way to explain this revolutionary concept to the pharaoh. This was a particularly difficult idea to communicate to someone who thought that *he* was the all-powerful master of the universe.

FORGET ABOUT A "QUICK FIX"

People who feel they are godlike tend to abuse others. They do not care about the feelings of other people, whom they consider inferior to themselves. This pharaoh had another personality problem as well—a lack of humility, which did not allow him to express gratitude. Just years earlier, Joseph had managed to save the pharaoh and all of Egypt, showing them how to prepare for seven years of famine. Once Egypt was saved, however, this pharaoh could not acknowledge that he had accepted the help of Joseph and the other Hebrews. Instead, he enslaved them, which convinced him yet again of his total control.

If the pharaoh had been a different sort of person, he would not have refused Moses and Aaron's request. If he had possessed even the slightest compassion, he could at least have granted the Israelites some temporary freedom, some dignity. But he did not. Compassion is one of the important lessons that the pharaoh— and all of us—have to learn. When others are under our control, we have to be particularly careful not to deny them their humanity.

I am reminded of this need every time that I walk through the hospital where I work. As I make my rounds, I see the patients' bill of rights posted throughout the units, but it is displayed most prominently in the locked mental health units, where patients do not have much control over their environment. This statement is a reminder that regardless of the condition of patients, they are entitled to certain basic rights and services, such as medical care, clothing, and meals. Most of all, they are entitled to respect as fellow human beings.

Respect means the ability to see another's point of view, even when it differs greatly from your own. That is another thing that the pharaoh failed to understand. Since he viewed himself as a god, he did not allow for any dissent. He regarded other people as beings who existed solely to serve him, and he valued them only for what they could do for him. He was not alone in feeling this way. But such an approach certainly cannot form the basis of a just society. So it is important for us to remember that when we *use* other people, we are not showing them respect. We are acting like the pharaoh.

To recognize the worth of other people, we first have to recognize our own worth, and then we need to acknowledge the spark of the Divine that exists in us and in others.

But the pharaoh, of course, did not recognize the spark of Israel's God—the One God—within himself, so he certainly could not perceive it in others. Even worse, his lack of compassion had drastic, immediate consequences. He quickly made life much more difficult for the Hebrews under his control, decreeing that the slaves no longer be given straw to make their bricks. Yet their daily brick production quota remained the same. Even though the Israelites worked hard trying to meet this impossible goal, they were, of course, unsuccessful, and were beaten for not completing their tasks on time. So the people went to Moses, crying in fear and in pain, asking why things had gotten worse, why their situation was more difficult than it had been before he came on the scene.

We learn something from this, too. Things typically get worse before they get better. Most people today—just like the ancient Israelites—want a quick fix for their problems. We would like to go to one doctor for one visit (with no waiting, of course), and get one prescription for one drug that will work the very first time we take it—with no side effects!

This attitude applies in psychotherapy, as well. Now that we are in an era of managed care, clients sometimes tell me that they hope to resolve all their issues in three or four sessions, since that is all their insurance plans will allow. I sometimes remind them of the complexity of counseling by asking, "Do you really think we can undo the patterns of twenty-five years of dysfunctional family life in three or four hours?"

As a clinical psychologist, I am keenly aware that there are no quick fixes. I am also very conscious of the fact that people in therapy naturally feel worse before they feel better. I think that a good analyst should be honest about this pattern during the first few sessions with a client.

But in ancient Egypt, there were no therapists to provide this perspective. And there were no quick fixes for the people, and none for the pharaoh. He had to learn slowly about a new and different God. No wonder he felt frustrated and bewildered. He only understood physical power, control, and intimidation. But Moses was trying to teach him about an invisible God, and how a Divine vision that is revealed to our unconscious can let us see other people and the world in a new way.

THE POWER OF EXPERIENCE

Human relationships are usually structured in one of two ways. As analyst Marion Woodman wrote in *The Pregnant Virgin,* they are based either on power and fear or on love, honor, and respect. The pharaoh was familiar with the path of power and fear. He needed to learn the path of God, the path of love, honor, and respect, but his harshness increased along with his stubbornness.

Even though Moses expected that it would be hard to get his message across, he was dismayed when his first effort at doing so led to new hardships for the Israelites. What is really interesting is that Moses had anticipated that his first intervention with the pharaoh would not succeed. Back at the burning bush, God had told Moses that the ruler of Egypt would not allow the Israelites to leave Egypt, not even for three days.

But knowing is not the same as experiencing. Sometimes we understand something intellectually, yet it is still incomprehensible to us when it actually occurs. Some years ago, a well-known psychiatrist was hospitalized at the medical center where I work. He had been diagnosed as having cancer. He knew that his illness was serious, and he wanted to know the details about his latest surgery. He asked his surgeon to report to him exactly what had been found and what the prognosis was. The pathology reports indicated that the cancer had invaded other sites in the patient's body, and his prognosis was unfavorable.

At first, the surgeon hesitated to heed his patient's request, but the psychiatrist convinced him that he was prepared to hear the whole truth. So the surgeon told it to him. Although the psychiatrist had all the scientific knowledge and years of analysis that he thought he needed to deal with this information, he could not take the news. He went into a major depression that severely affected the quality of the rest of his life.

So experience is central and words are incredibly significant. It is not just what we hear, but how things are told to us that makes the difference. As one of my students told me, "words have a long half-life." I agree.

Even though Moses knew how the pharaoh would respond to his request, he could not deal with the suffering that he witnessed. So he asked God why he had been selected for this failed mission. He also asked why God had allowed the Israelites' condition to worsen.

God responded that Moses would witness continued Divine intervention in the process of the Israelites' redemption. The pharaoh's reeducation would continue, since he had such difficulty comprehending the new concepts that Moses had tried to teach him. The next part of the lesson would be conducted in language that the pharaoh already understood. The process would be long, painful, difficult—and extremely intriguing.

CHAPTER 10

Transformation

M OSES HAD A VERY DIFFICULT time accepting the failure
of his first intervention with the pharaoh. After Moses
lamented to God that his actions had only made things worse,
God appeared to him again, reassuring Moses and reminding
him of the unbreakable covenant with Abraham, Isaac, Jacob,
and all of their descendants. God said, "I have heard the groan-
ing of the children of Israel, whom the Egyptians keep in
bondage; and I have remembered my covenant. . . . I will bring
you out from under the burdens of the Egyptians." God was saying to Moses and all the Israelites that they would never be abandoned, that God would always remain true to His word.

Moses conveyed this message of hope to the Israelites, but it
fell on deaf ears. The spirit of the slaves was so crushed, and they
were so exhausted from their labors, that no words could comfort them.

Although Moses was unable to get through to his people at
this time, he did not lose hope. God had made Moses realize that
a mission often requires many trials before it is successful. Moses
knew that he and Aaron must confront the pharaoh once again.
They would now try to get through to him in a language that he

definitely understood—magic. After all, magicians and sorcerers were an integral part of the Egyptian court. So when Moses and Aaron appeared before the pharaoh, they brought their own "magic"—symbolized by the rod that God directed them to use.

Coming before the pharaoh's throne, Aaron cast the rod down on the ground, where it was transformed into a snake. Alarmed, the pharaoh called his wise men and sorcerers, who sneered at Moses and Aaron and promptly re-created this wonder, using their own magical arts. Then came the moment of truth as to who possessed the superior power. Aaron grabbed his snake and it became a rod once again. The magicians were not intimidated, and they did the same. But then something astonishing happened: the rod of Aaron and Moses came to life and swallowed the rods of all the magicians.

This is a powerful and vivid story. It is no wonder that so many of us remember it in detail from our childhood Bible classes. But a central element in this episode is rarely, if ever, addressed. Why does pharaoh's lesson involve a snake? What is so special about this particular symbol? I believe that the snake teaches the pharaoh, as well as the rest of us, something very important—our ability to change. Snakes shed their skin so they can grow, and they become renewed in the process. Thus, they symbolize rebirth, renewal, and creative energy.

Furthermore, just as change is a natural process in the life of the serpent, it can be in our lives as well. Just as a snake naturally sheds its skin, we are each naturally capable of shedding our old ways and attitudes, reemerging as more developed human beings. As James Redfield said in *The Tenth Insight,* all of life is a process of continuous rebirth. Moreover, I believe very strongly that change is possible for every person. Yet, the vast majority of people whom I have encountered believe that such transformation is virtually impossible. They sigh that "a leopard can't change its spots," or "you can't teach an old dog new tricks." *That* is what they have come to believe, that their circumstances—family dysfunction, trauma, genetics—have shaped them in such a way that leaves little or no room for them to behave differently.

STAYING AWAY FROM TOXICITY TRANSFORMS US

But life changes are always possible. Moses was a prime example of that. He started out as a stutterer who felt incapable of speaking to the pharaoh. But over the course of his mission to Egypt and the rest of his life—as he became more and more of a leader—his self-confidence grew dramatically. By the end of the Torah, he had become a fluent speaker, whose lengthy farewell address fills almost the entire book of Deuteronomy.

What was true for Moses can be true for the rest of us. Many of my clients experience personal growth and change, and along the way, they notice this process reflected in their dreams, which frequently include snakes. Numerous times, clients have described dreams involving a frightening serpent. Yet, by the end of analysis, those same clients have often reported dreams in which they are playing with snakes and are unafraid of them. That which was terrifying—a venomous snake—has now become a friend.

The process of analysis leading to increased self-knowledge is long and tedious. I often think of it as the task of unearthing ancient artifacts that lie beneath the surface. In 1967, I was privileged to participate in an archaeological dig at the top of Masada in Israel. Everyone on the team was given a small digging tool, which we were trained to use. But we were also cautioned to proceed very slowly and carefully. If we went too fast, we might break the very items we were trying to uncover.

Freud understood very well the parallel between psychoanalysis and discovering archaeological artifacts. In his consulting room in Vienna, he and his patients were surrounded by his collection of thousands of ancient figurines and vases from Egypt, Greece, and the Far East. While conducting his analytic sessions, he was acutely aware of his attempts to bring to light the patient's relics of the past, and he proceeded very carefully and sensitively.

But sometimes unearthing the past is not enough. In order to stop repeating old patterns of behavior, it is often necessary to physically relocate, at least temporarily; to remove yourself from the toxicity that surrounds you and place yourself in a nourishing, nurturing milieu. If it is impossible to get away physically, it is still possible to remove yourself psychically from the poisonous atmosphere around you.

Many of the greatest characters in the Bible had to leave their families and their homelands to begin life anew and fulfill their personal destinies. The patriarch Abraham, for example, had to remove himself from his idolatrous home and country so he could found a new people. God told him, "Go forth from your native land, from your birthplace, and from your father's house to the land that I will show you." It took a tremendous amount of faith for Abraham to heed this Divine call and journey to a land that was completely unknown to him, a place where he could completely transform his life.

Healing is *only* possible when transformation occurs. In fact, that is the message of the caduceus—the symbol of medicine that, of course, portrays snakes. It tells us that we need to confront the serpent—the toxicity and darkness in ourselves and in those around us. Only then can we shed our old perceptions and attitudes, enabling us to be renewed and to experience healing.

But what about that feeling of dread about doing or seeing things in a new way? That is the price we pay for learning how to transform ourselves—the acceptance that life is made up of uncertainty and struggle. The only thing of which we can be certain is uncertainty. Life is a pendulum, constantly swinging between birth and death, light and dark, health and illness, masculine and feminine. We experience life at every point along this constantly shifting continuum.

As we have seen, the pharaoh could not accept a world of

change and uncertainty. He was fearful and insecure and needed to be sure of his absolute power. He could not even accept his own human frailties, because if he were not a supreme power, then things could happen that were not subject to his control. Since the pharaoh could not confront his fears and would not admit his vulnerability, he again refused to let the Israelites go.

Trying new forms of communication did not work with him. The lesson of personal transformation was lost on him. A new, radical approach was needed—powerful, deadly plagues.

CHAPTER 11

Destruction and Creation

W<small>E ALL KNOW ABOUT THE TEN</small> plagues and the destruction they caused. The Nile first turns to blood, then becomes filled with frogs, which invade every house in the land; lice infest people and animals; wild animals overrun the country; pestilence strikes the Egyptians' livestock; humans and beasts suffer severe boils on their skin; hail devastates the countryside; locusts destroy whatever the hail has not wiped out; three days of intense darkness paralyze Egypt; and finally, all the firstborn Egyptian males die.

That is an awesome list of calamities. I have struggled with the why and wherefore of these plagues, particularly with the last. Even on Passover, which celebrates the deliverance of the Israelites from servitude, I am troubled when I realize that innocent children died so others could be saved. According to the Midrash, some Egyptians died during *each* of the ten plagues, not just during the final calamity. The rabbis were aware of the conflict that we feel when reading about the deaths of the Egyptians. That is why they devised a significant ritual during the Passover *seder* that highlights the importance of sensitivity to another's pain. In keeping with this tradition, as my family and I recite each of the plagues during our *seder*, the evening ceremony that begins Passover, we spill some wine out of our goblets to remind ourselves that our joy cannot be complete while others, even our enemies, suffer and die.

Even with this realization, we each struggle to understand the suffering of the innocent. One of my therapy clients, Saul, expressed himself quite clearly on this subject. He said, "Rabbi, I must be frank with you. That whole episode in Genesis of Abraham being told to sacrifice his son Isaac has always bothered me. If Abraham had gone ahead and destroyed Isaac, that would have created an enormous crisis of faith for me."

Then, Saul continued, "That last plague in Egypt, when all the firstborn Egyptians die. I have tremendous difficulty accepting that Divine judgment. If that kind of punishment could happen—even to an enemy—it could happen to anyone." Saul and I have continued to explore these feelings, which ultimately led to discussing the light—and the shadow—side of God.

FINDING GOOD BY SURVIVING EVIL

I don't have easy answers for Saul. I don't even have them for myself. However, just this past year, as I reviewed the stories in Genesis and Exodus again, I gained some insights that have helped me understand this difficult text.

I have come to realize how important it is to view the Torah as an integrated whole, rather than to focus only on a particular verse or chapter that we may find troubling. Such a limited focus produces a kind of biblical tunnel vision that lets us see only a narrow picture, rather than the entire visual field.

I believe that it is necessary to look at the entire Bible—from the beginning—so we can refocus our vision and gain greater perspective, particularly on such pivotal episodes as the Egyptian plagues. To understand what happened in Egypt, we need to explore the development of human nature, as well as past Divine promises.

At the beginning of Genesis, God decided to create human beings, creatures imbued with a Divine spirit and free will—the ability to make decisions, to distinguish between right and wrong, and to choose accordingly.

But this bold endeavor did not succeed right away. Even in Paradise, things did not work out well. There were only two people in the Garden of Eden, Adam and Eve, and they had only one commandment to keep: not to eat from the tree of knowledge of good and evil. Yet, problems arose. Many of my students complain about the difficulties of observing the 613 Jewish commandments. But Adam and Eve had just one commandment—and they couldn't even manage that! So they were expelled from Eden and things went from bad to worse. Eventually, everyone on earth became so corrupt that God actually regretted having created humans.

This Divine regret may be difficult for us to understand. During my years as a therapist, I have counseled families who tearfully regretted that a particular child had been born. Usually, these parents are dismayed at having produced a child who does not live up to their expectations or desires. For example, one mother told me that ever since she learned that her daughter was addicted to alcohol and other drugs, she could not accept her any more as her own flesh and blood. She was now some sort of aberration who had appeared out of nowhere.

But after the expulsion from the Garden of Eden, God's reaction went beyond regret. He came to a startling realization: "The Lord saw that the wickedness of man was great in the earth, and that every inclination of the thoughts of his heart was only evil continually." So God decided to completely destroy all that had been created—not only people, but all that had been put on earth, including plant life, animals, and birds. One exception was made: Noah, who had found favor in God's eyes.

Noah was directed to build an ark that would carry him, his family, and pairs of every animal species to safety during a great

flood. After the waters receded, God recognized that human nature was the same as it had been before the flood, "for the inclination of man's heart is evil from his youth." Yet, God promised
to never "again destroy every living being."

To help humans rebuild their ruined world, God laid down a
number of universal principles that they had to obey, including
prohibitions against murder and oppression.

So God tried again to shape people who would not act op-
pressively or tolerate such behavior in others—people who would
be kind, sensitive, caring, and compassionate.

God decided to create a new people to serve as role models to
help all others through the struggles of life. A covenant was made
with Abraham and his descendants. They would be a light unto
the nations—a blessing to all. But striving to bring more light into
the world would be a tremendous challenge and a huge responsibility. Moreover, the covenant included some very frightening
aspects. As God told Abraham: "Know for sure that your seed will
be strangers in a land that is not theirs, and shall serve them; and
they shall afflict them four hundred years; and also that nation,
whom they shall serve, will I judge; and afterward they shall
come out with great possession."

I often wonder how any of us would respond to such an agree-
ment with God. I have actually asked members of my Bible study
class about this. "Suppose," I said, " you were told that your descendants would become a great and successful people. But first
your children and grandchildren would have to go through terrible times of slavery and oppression. Would any of you agree to
such a proposal?" The vast majority of my students say they
could never condemn their children to suffer, even though the
end result would be positive.

So how could Abraham agree to this arrangement? I believe
that he understood the message that God was really conveying
to him: when you strive to be good and carry out God's mission,
other people will not make it easy for you. You will be treated like

strangers, you will be enslaved by others, and you will be afflicted. Yet, Abraham does not hesitate to accept this precious covenant.

SAVING OURSELVES BY SAVING OTHERS

And that brings us back to the pharaoh and the experience of the Israelites in Egypt. When the Egyptians oppressed the Israelites, they violated basic, Divine rules governing human behavior. Since the pharaoh and his people were breaking these fundamental laws, they had to be punished.

Initially, God seemed to be "constrained" while reacting to the Egyptians. After all, God had promised to never again destroy all of humanity, even when oppression and corruption were overtaking the world. But God could take decisive, instructive action. This time, the entire world would not be destroyed, only part of the nation that had brought so much suffering to the Israelites. God would demonstrate to the Egyptians—and to all the world—that Divine force can create, but also destroy when such action is warranted.

Creation followed the order described at the beginning of Genesis, culminating with the highest form of life—humans. The destruction in Egypt culminated in the *death* of the Egyptian firstborn, just as the pinnacle of creation had been the *birth* of humanity. Here we have creation in reverse, but only the Egyptians were afflicted. The rest of the world was saved from annihilation because of the Divine promise to spare it.

This is a very difficult and sobering lesson. The truth is that anyone or any nation violating the terms of a covenant with God is subject to destruction. If the Hebrews did not live up to God's covenant with Abraham, they too would face annihilation. But there is hope as well. The only reason that creation is sustained is the existence of people who help others out of their own personal "Egypts" (difficult times) and do not oppress others. Therefore, we are all responsible not only for each other, but also for the maintenance of the world as we know it.

Each of us has silent partners to help us along. According to the Midrash, in every generation, thirty-six wholly righteous individuals help the oppressed. On their behalf, the world is sustained. None of us knows who they are. *They* do not even know who they are! And I have some interesting news. If you even think that you are one of them, you are automatically disqualified!

Although we may not be completely righteous, many of us find that sometimes our own suffering increases our empathy and understanding, and leads to improvement in our actions. That is one of the principal lessons of the servitude in Egypt, a lesson that the Hebrews were commanded to never forget. The central message of the Torah is the continual reminder that since we know what it is like to be afflicted, we must not hurt others. Rather, we should be especially sensitive to the stranger and anyone else who might be the victim of oppression.

I understand and accept that message, yet I still have difficulty comprehending why we must sometimes undergo painful experiences to gain empathy for the plight of others. However, two of my colleagues have deepened my understanding of this issue. Both are retired physicians in their seventies—one is a cardiologist; the other, a neurosurgeon. In recent years, both have undergone heart bypass operations.

The cardiologist's experience changed him dramatically. "I've always considered myself an excellent physician," he said, "and my colleagues agree that I'm a brilliant diagnostician. But if, during all these years, I had understood what being a patient was really like, I would have practiced medicine in a totally different way. I now find that it's not only the big things—the academic or procedural issues that we doctors spend so much time on—that are so important. It's the little things, like how you feel when you're half-naked in a backless hospital gown and have to call the nurse to help you with a bedpan. You feel such a loss of dignity and self. I never fully appreciated that."

His colleague, the neurosurgeon, had a similar revelation after his own hospital experience. "Most people think of me as an outstanding doctor," he told me. "But recently, I have come to understand something that I never did before. I've always looked at the patient's chart and evaluated major symptoms and complaints. But I never *listened* adequately. I never understood that the patient was struggling to communicate his or her feelings and fears. I never heard the message behind the words, behind the frightened looks."

Both of these exceptional individuals learned something positive from their pain. Can any other good come from a terrible experience, such as the Egyptian slavery? I still search for my own answers, but one of my students, Ben, offered an interesting response to this complex question.

"Suppose," he said one day in class, "a newly married husband and wife set off on a honeymoon journey aboard their yacht. For four weeks they eat, drink, and enjoy a succession of pleasures with each other. Then they return home. At the end of the month, if you measure the bond between them, it will certainly be strong and loving.

"But now, suppose that this same couple encounters stormy weather during their cruise. Even worse, they become marooned on a deserted island. They have to depend on each other as they hunt, fish, build shelter, and fight for their survival. After a month, they are rescued. How deep do you think their bond will be after all they have endured together? Don't you think that it will be even stronger and deeper than in the first example?"

I understand Ben's point. Perhaps the period of enslavement in Egypt helped bring the Israelites not only closer to one another, but to God as well.

In any event, the time for their liberation had not yet arrived. They continued to serve their Egyptian taskmasters. And in the darkness of their servitude, they anxiously looked for the light.

CHAPTER 12

Darkness and Light

As the Israelites eagerly awaited their redemption, they witnessed a succession of plagues that paralyzed and destroyed Egypt. Each plague sent a particular message to the pharaoh and the Egyptians about the limits of their control over creation. Finally, the ninth plague—darkness—arrived, teaching the Israelites, the Egyptians—and all of us today—a great lesson about our inner and outer lives.

The Bible describes this plague very vividly: "And the Lord said to Moses: 'Stretch out your hand toward heaven, that there may be darkness over the land of Egypt, even darkness which may be felt.' . . . And there was a thick darkness in all the land of Egypt three days."

All of us have experienced varying degrees of darkness. My family and I have spent some vacation time in the mountains, where no electric lights illuminated the paths around our cabin at night. When no moon was visible, the night was very dark indeed.

But such celestial conditions alone cannot fully explain the plague of darkness. For one thing, it is described in a way that is difficult to comprehend, a darkness that could be *felt*. Furthermore, the Midrash uses the following language to describe this darkness: "Even if the Egyptians had brought in all the candles and all the wicks in the world, these would not have provided light for them."

From this description, it is clear that we are not talking about physical darkness and light. But what other kind is there? As I pointed out in chapter 2, the story of creation begins with God's saying, "Let there be light." This means that a Divine energy, a radiance, is reflected in our own zest for life. When that life force is absent, we plunge into the darkness of despair and despondency.

That was what happened to the Egyptians. Their state of mind was abundantly clear. They "saw not one another, neither rose any from his place for three days; but all of the children of Israel had light in their dwellings." The Egyptians could not *see* each other during this period. Most of us recognize that when we are completely engrossed in our own darkness, we cannot see beyond our own boundaries and needs. That is what the Egyptians experienced. Consequently, they did not visit their friends—they did not have any social contact with others—for three days. This is not a case of external darkness, but of internal despair. The biblical description of this darkness resonates with anyone who has ever experienced depression, which most of us have in one way or another. Many people go around with "walking depression," yet function quite well. This type of depression is so common and so undetectable by others that it often goes undiagnosed, even though it makes life difficult for the person afflicted with it.

OUR INDIVIDUAL LIGHT
CAN VANQUISH DEPRESSION

Depression can also manifest itself in a severe and disabling way, like this Egyptian "darkness." One of my former clients, Susan, described her experience with clinical depression this way: "As much as I try to tell you exactly how I felt, you can't possibly understand it. Only if you've been through it yourself can you have any inkling of what I'm talking about. Imagine going through every moment of every day without the ability to experience any pleasure. You can't sleep, and you toss and turn, waiting for the morning.

"And then, when everyone else is getting out of bed, you really have no reason to join them. There is nothing to look forward to, no hope that things will ever get any better. You don't feel like eating or doing anything, and simply trying to sleep to escape this dark pain is nearly impossible. You can't even talk without crying, and if you take a pill, it only brings temporary relief. You don't feel up to visiting with anybody, even good friends who want to come over and cheer you up. And you don't feel like ever leaving the house again."

Susan's comments resonate with the effect that the ninth plague had on the Egyptians. They became so engrossed with themselves that they could not even think about other people, let alone visit them. All they could do was remain—immobilized and despondent—in their homes.

During this same period, however, the Israelites experienced light in their dwellings. Furthermore, the Midrash tells us that if an Israelite and an Egyptian were walking side by side, the Egyptian would experience only inner darkness, while the Israelite would experience internal light. That was truly a miracle, given the norms of human behavior. Depression can be contagious, and people suffering from it typically do not want those around them to be happy. Thus, when the Israelites were *not* sucked into their neighbors' dark state of mind, they were overcoming something as firmly established as a basic law of physics, like gravity. It is as if my pencil were to "drop" up instead of down.

In addition to appreciating this contravention of natural law, I cannot help noticing the tremendous irony in this plague. I picture an Israelite and an Egyptian walking side by side. Their situations have become completely reversed. The Egyptian oppressor, who has done everything to remove all light from the Israelite's life, is plunged into darkness and despair. At the same time, the Israelite, whose spirits should have been completely crushed by the harsh servitude, experiences zest, hope, and motivation.

That internal light experienced by the Israelites continues to manifest itself today. Each of us is capable of sharing in it when we let ourselves be conduits for sparks of the Divine. That can seem like a lofty, unattainable goal until we realize just how achievable it can be.

To help explain this idea a little more clearly, let me tell you about Rabbi Abraham Isaac Kook (1865–1935), the first Ashkenazi chief rabbi of Palestine before the state of Israel was established. Rabbi Kook was a brilliant philosopher and religious leader. He was also a great mystic and prolific author. The titles of many of his works include the word *orot*, which means "lights."

Why did he use that term so often? I believe that it tells us a great deal about how he viewed himself and his teachings. When he wrote or spoke, he realized that he was acting as the transmitter of light and knowledge from above. He saw himself as a vehicle through which the Divine spirit could illuminate many existential dilemmas. He recognized that his words and teachings flowed from his Higher Self—his illuminated unconscious—rather than from his ego.

As a consequence of this point of view, Rabbi Kook saw the light inside every human being. He valued all people, regardless of their background or denomination. He respected people of all faiths. We can all act in the manner of Rabbi Kook. Once we let that illumination from above pervade ourselves, we can view other people and events from a different perspective. We will no longer be caught up in strivings of the ego, such as our drives toward power and control, nor will we disdain others who are different from us.

By contrast, the "pharaoh mentality" is always characterized by inner darkness. A pharaoh-type cannot be happy even when things go right for him. He sees himself as a perpetual victim, and he looks for the cloud in every silver lining. He cannot take pleasure in another's glory or rejoice at someone else's good fortune. My client Martin is such a person. He has a number of legitimate concerns, including being unemployed for the past year and a half. But to hear him talk, you would imagine that he is the victim of a widespread conspiracy to keep him down. As he sees it, his former employer did not live up to his promises and played favorites, keeping someone else employed while letting Martin go. Members of his church don't respect him, and his kids' teachers pay no attention to his suggestions. One thing is clear. Martin is not experiencing any internal light.

Most of us try to put more light into our lives. Some of us move to Malibu, hoping that a glass-enclosed living room with an ocean view will bathe us in light. Others redecorate and refurbish their homes, assuming that new furniture or brighter colors will bring the light they seek. But none of these strategies will bring the light that really matters—the light within. And when we see people who seem to have this, some of us might act like the Egyptians. We notice that others have light in their dwellings, while we have none in ours, and we want to pull them down into our despair.

But the experience of the Israelites teaches us an important lesson. Despite the despair of their servitude and the external, harsh aspects of their lives, they could maintain their zest for life and the ability to look beyond their immediate situation. Each of us can experience that same blessing. The choice is ours. As a patient taking his first step following hip surgery said, "I'm happier being happy than being sad."

Oddly enough, it is often right in the middle of the darkness—at night while we sleep—that visions of light arise from deep within us. These dreams, which always include visual images, tell us that some inner light exists within us. All of us experience this light in the midst of darkness on a regular basis. In fact, we often have several dreams in one night.

This human ability to transcend darkness is also made clear to me when I view the paintings of the German artist Peter Birkhauser. When I look at his vivid, haunting, sometimes startling images, I am acutely aware that these visions arose from the dark side of his unconscious. Birkhauser's decision to bring them to the light of art has produced something constructive and wonderful for himself, as well as for those of us who appreciate his work. By doing this, he illuminates the darkness for himself and for others. I appreciate his contribution to my life every time I look through a book of his paintings, which is aptly entitled *Light from the Darkness*.

Some people imagine that since I work in a major medical center, I am surrounded only by darkness—major illness, pain, suffering, and death. Almost every week, at least one person asks me, "How can you take it, day after day?" But I assure my friends that I find a lot of light. Most patients get better and return home. Even in those cases when a patient dies, I find light and comfort in the hope that, through our mutual sharing, such individuals were helped along their spiritual journey.

HOLINESS CAN FOLLOW SORROW

The plague of darkness can teach us many positive lessons. The Egyptians' inability to see one another tells us about the despair that enveloped them. But this also conveys another idea. When we do not truly *see* someone else, it may be because we do not see the godliness in that person or in ourselves. Unfortunately, that unseeing attitude—that narcissism—is too prevalent in our society today. We have to remind ourselves *not* to act like the ancient Egyptians, but to recognize other people and their needs.

Now that we understand the nature of this darkness, we need to go a step further. Why did this biblical plague continue for three days? The answer is suggested in what the entire Israelite nation would soon be told: "This month shall be *unto you* the beginning of months." Doesn't it seem strange that the calendar was being discussed at a time like this, when the Israelites were still enslaved? They were not free, their time was not even their own, yet they were told that the months will be "unto you"—that is, theirs to determine. What does this mean?

The message is that whenever you experience enslavement or any other type of darkness, you often *imagine* that freedom will solve all your problems. But this will not happen. Even while enjoying freedom, you will experience the cyclical nature of life. The moon will continue to wax and wane, so that even when you think you are in charge of your own calendar, take note of the fact that, at times, the moon will eventually become less visible, and you will experience more darkness. In fact, for three days each month—right before the appearance of the new moon—you will not see any of the moon in the night sky.

The sooner that we accept the fact that life goes in cycles, the happier we will be. No matter how long our personal darkness lasts, we eventually see a sliver of light above us. This understanding can elevate our spirits and help us get through the cycle ahead.

It also helps to remember that we are never alone during these cycles. As Oscar Wilde wrote in *De Profundis*, "Where there is sorrow, there is holy ground."

We can also derive strength from the realization that we are all a part of a cycle of history that spans adversity and joy. We need to explore where we have come from if we are to understand where we are going. Then we will know that true freedom is not attained merely by fleeing our captors and oppressors. It comes only when we have cast off our own yokes of psychic enslavement.

CHAPTER 13

Gifts

THE STORY OF THE ISRAELITES' enslavement and journey to
freedom is really quite puzzling. Even though we are familiar with the plagues and the pharaoh's eventual decision to let the
people go, when we read some of the pertinent biblical verses,
we cannot help but wonder just what was really going on.

We know about the harshness of the Egyptian servitude. The
Egyptians "made the children of Israel to serve with crushing
oppression. And they made their lives bitter with hard work." We
have a pretty clear picture of the misery that the Israelites endured. As if the physical labors of enslavement were not enough,
the Hebrews had had to watch all their male infants cast into the
river!

After Moses's first intervention on behalf of his people, their
situation grew even more intolerable. They were expected to
make their daily quota of bricks, even when the raw material—
straw—was no longer provided for them. Then they were beaten
for not producing as many bricks as before! No wonder their
spirits became so crushed that they could not even listen to
Moses's message of hope the next time he came to see them.

These images are made real to me during each Passover *seder*.

When I was very young, the pictures in the *Haggadah* (the prayer book for the Passover home ceremony) of Egyptian taskmasters beating the Hebrew slaves helped me realize what such suffering was actually like. Even as an adult, I often focus on such images during the *seder*.

But in recent years, I have begun to pay more attention to other descriptions of the interactions between the Egyptians and the Israelites. For example, long before the Hebrews were freed, God told Moses: "I will give this people favor in the sight of the Egyptians. And it shall come to pass that, when you go, you will not go empty; but every woman shall ask of her neighbor, and of the one in whose house she resides, jewels of silver, and jewels of gold, and garments; and you shall put them upon your sons, and upon your daughters."

This is an interesting portrait of the daily lives of the Israelites during their period of slavery. We know that most of them lived in the province of Goshen, an area set apart from the rest of the Egyptian populace. But these verses say that some Israelites actually lived in the homes of their taskmasters, where they worked as servants.

This understanding presents us with a very valuable lesson about how to treat domestic workers. Many people in my community in West Los Angeles rely on outside help in their homes, and quite a few of these housekeepers live with their employers for most of the week. Over the years, it has become clear to me who treats their help as the Egyptians did, and who consciously tries *not* to behave this way.

Maria, whom I see at a Los Angeles free mental-health clinic, has the misfortune of being employed by people who do not treat her properly. Unfortunately, due to her economic and immigration status, she cannot easily leave that family. Listen as she describes what her life is like: "These are not bad people, and everyone likes them, but they make me feel so bad. They never even say my name! When someone comes in the door, they say, 'My girl will help you with your coat!' And I'm not even a girl—I'm a grandmother. But that's not the worst thing. It's like I'm not even there. You would not believe it, but the other night, while I am cleaning the room, the mister sits on the couch with his wife, and they begin to sort of play with each other, if you know what I mean—kissing, hugging, touching in different places, undressing. I am so embarrassed to see people behaving like that. But they don't care. I'm just invisible—not even a real person to them!"

These employers don't know what a dehumanizing environment they are creating for their housekeeper. And they don't know that when they behave this way, they are acting like the ancient Egyptians, although in a slightly more benign manner.

By contrast, I enjoy visiting the Smiths, whose helper Bernice has been a loyal, trusted, and respected employee for several years. She is always addressed by name, demonstrating that she is valued as a fellow human being. She eats with the family. They always celebrate her birthday and other special occasions with a small party—complete with cake and gifts—in her honor. She knows that she is appreciated for the important contribution that she makes to her employers' lives. Their children have absorbed this lesson well. From an early age, they knew that they had to respect Bernice as they respect any adult. This is a home that will produce people who do not subjugate or demean others.

DOING GOOD DESTROYS HATE

The description of Egyptian-Israelite interactions offers other important insights. For example, we learn something from the way the Israelites are told to ask for gifts from their enslavers. What is particularly striking is that re'ehu, (meaning "friend") is the Hebrew word used for the Egyptians, indicating that the Israelites ask for gifts from people they now regard as their *friends!*

That is pretty amazing. It is even more difficult to understand when we consider that these words directly precede the warning that the Egyptian firstborn are about to be slain! Yet, God's promise to make the Hebrews find favor in the sight of the Egyptians has come true—even at this time!

Even *after* the Egyptian firstborn have died, their families give the Israelites jewels of silver and of gold, and garments. The Bible informs us that "the Lord gave the people favor in the sight of the Egyptians, so that they let them have what they asked."

Surprisingly enough, we are told that by receiving these material gifts, the Israelites "save" the Egyptians. How can we possibly understand that statement? To appreciate what is going on, we need to consider the covenant that God made with Abraham and his descendants. Long ago, Abraham was told: "Know for sure that your seed will be strangers in a land that is not theirs, and shall serve them; and they shall afflict them four hundred years, and also that nation, whom they shall serve, will I judge; and afterward they shall come out with great possession." Just as enslavement was part of the initial prophecy, so too was God's intention that the people would leave Egypt with precious gifts.

But to really understand these biblical references to leaving Egypt with items of value, we need to compare them with a later biblical message concerning the freeing of a Hebrew slave. No Hebrew could keep a slave longer than seven years, and when that slave left the house of his master, he could *not* be sent away empty-handed. Rather, the Bible commands, "you shall furnish him liberally out of your flock, and out of your threshing-floor, and out of your winepress." Such gifts would indicate your appreciation for services performed. They would also demonstrate that you respect the humanity and dignity of the servant who is leaving your employ. These are the types of gifts of appreciation that the Egyptians also had to give the Israelites.

So the Egyptians were not such complete tyrants after all. I find it particularly significant that after their Exodus from Egypt, the Hebrews were constantly reminded, "And you shall remember that you were a servant in the land of Egypt, and the Lord your God redeemed you." Furthermore, you are *not* to hate the Egyptians, despite all that they did: "You shall not abhor an Egyptian, because you were a stranger in his land."

These various statements seem to create a paradox. We are told over and over again to *remember* the experience in Egypt. Yet we are not to harbor ill feelings toward the Egyptians. So exactly how are we to recall the experience? One thing seems clear. We are to remember in such a way that we learn a great moral lesson from this episode, taking care that our own behavior is never like that of the Egyptians. To paraphrase philosopher George Santayana, we have to remember the slavery so as not to inflict it upon others.

The Bible is telling us that there is a new way to remember. Rather than focusing on the atrocities and tragedies that have befallen us, we should behave in the *opposite* manner than the Egyptians did. Spending our days and nights hating the Egyptians means that we completely miss the essence of this episode. Furthermore, if our hatred goes unchecked, it will destroy us. So the proper way for us to remember is to do good.

Unfortunately, many of my psychotherapy clients have lost this essential battle with themselves. They fail to realize, as M. Scott Peck explains in *The Road Less Traveled*, that forgiveness is selfish. We forgive other people not only for *their* sake, but also for *our own*. Hating is self-destructive and a waste of energy. As a divorced woman once told me, "I don't hate my ex-husband. If I did, I might as well have stayed married to him!" Her point was well made. She had to bid farewell not only to the house that they shared, but also to the strong emotions that he evoked in her.

Some people I know provide courageous examples of how to remember. For example, Ruth, a Holocaust survivor, has incorporated this understanding into her own life. "I have never hated," she told me, "so I did not transmit hate to my son."

That is a remarkable achievement. So many people pass on

their hatred, fears, and sadness to future generations. While I understand the causes of this, I can see that these people are transmitting damage, not healing. By contrast, someone like Ruth has a positive view of the world, which she has conveyed to her family. I am deeply touched when I hear this woman who has witnessed so much horror express her belief that people are essentially more good than bad.

REMEMBERING WHO WE ARE

So we need to remember, but in the right way. That helps us understand how, by accepting gifts from them, the Israelites saved the Egyptians. They saved them by not keeping vindictiveness in their hearts. They saved them by focusing on the good that they did, not the evil.

Remembering can also help us save and heal ourselves. One essential thing that the Israelites were to remember was their rebirth as a free nation. That is why they are told, on the eve of their liberation, "This month shall be unto you the beginning of months." Since their journey to freedom would take place in the springtime, that season would forever be celebrated as the "birthday" of the people. However, their calendar year, which marks the chronology from the beginning of the world, would begin earlier, in the fall, at Rosh Hashanah, the Jewish New Year.

These two celebrations reflect the fact that most of us celebrate more than one occasion. Certainly, we all recognize our chronological milestones, such as birthdays, and celebrate them annually. But I would guess that nearly every one of us commemorates at least one other special day each year that marks some new beginning or understanding for ourselves, a time when we followed through on some resolution or made some significant move in our lives.

Steve, for instance, told me that his real birthday was the date he entered psychoanalysis. For my colleague Shari, it was when she finished therapy. For George, it was when he took out a bank loan and opened his own business. And for Sharon, it was "a moment when I truly experienced God, a Divine spiritual awakening and realization that has changed my entire life."

Even Gilda, who'd had an abusive childhood, was able to celebrate her "rebirth-day"—the day she left her family's house. She feels that she now understands her parents and does not hate them, even though they "enslaved" her.

It is interesting that these people have incorporated other lessons of the Exodus into their everyday lives. They understand better than most that the descendants of the enslaved Israelites have to learn more than how to refrain from being vindictive. They must also be particularly sensitive, caring, and empathetic.

We can all try to integrate these important qualities. In Los Angeles, where I live, I see a tremendous need for understanding among Jews, as well as between people of various faiths and cultures. In recent years, waves of immigrants have come here from many lands, including Russia, Israel, and Iran. We who are already here, especially those of us who immigrated from elsewhere in the United States or Europe, should know the right way to act. After all, we have been told—numerous times—to remember that we too were once strangers in the land of Egypt. One would think that this sensitivity would carry over into our actions and we would immediately reach out in friendship to these newcomers who are now strangers in our land.

Sadly, this is not the general rule. Many nice people whom I know find it easier to focus on cultural differences and language barriers than on the commonalties they share with these new residents. It never ceases to amaze me that when strangers meet— in Los Angeles, New York, or Jerusalem—they immediately bond when they learn that they both came from the same city. They start to speak in a loving, effusive manner: "Oh, you're from Warsaw! My family lived there for generations. You must have gone to school with my sister." But that same excitement is rarely present when they meet someone from a faraway community—such as Kiev or Teheran—even though that person is just as much a brother or a sister.

The essential task for each of us is to remember and recognize that everyone we meet was once a stranger. That recognition will enable us to act in a welcoming, caring fashion. As that beautiful song from the musical *The Fantastiks* reminds us, "Try to remember, and if you remember, then follow."

CHAPTER 14

Why Is This Night Different?

A T EVERY PASSOVER *seder,* the youngest person at our family's table asks the Four Questions. Perhaps the most famous of these is, "Why is this night different from all other nights?"

That question is central to the ritual of the *seder* night, which is referred to in the Bible as "a night of [God's] watching." On this night of God's protection, some families of patients stay over at the hospital where I work in order to celebrate Passover with those who are dear to them. They are acting in the manner of God, demonstrating their watchfulness over their loved ones.

But what is it about this night that makes it so different, so special? Well, on this date—the fifteenth of the Hebrew month of Nisan, the anniversary of the Exodus from Egypt—the moon is always full. The message seems to be that as we are celebrating Passover here on earth, God is shining Divine light and protection from above.

There are other answers as well, and I believe that they are related to the Passover offering of a lamb that was sacrificed on the night of the departure from Egypt. Everyone could participate in eating this sacrifice—men and women, Israelites, strangers, and converts—but the common requirement for all the males was that they be circumcised first. The Israelites were to take blood and put it on their doorposts and then eat the sacrifice, along with *matzoh* (unleavened bread) and bitter herbs. What kind of unusual ritual was taking place here, and why was the placing of blood necessary? And why are we told that "the blood will be *to you* for a sign"? How and why will it be a sign "to you"?

To answer these questions, we have to think about what the Israelites had been doing until now, aside from their labors as slaves. After Moses's first unsuccessful intervention with the pharaoh, they no longer listened to him because of their low spirits and depression. Furthermore, during the previous nine plagues, God had done all the work! They had been merely passive observers.

So at this point, before the tenth plague—the slaying of the Egyptian firstborn—God seemed to be saying, "I will redeem you, but this will require one monumental act on your part. Take a lamb—one of the Egyptian deities—and slaughter it. Then put blood on your door where it will be visible to all, demonstrating that you are rejecting the god of the Egyptians and showing obedience to Me."

IS ACTION STRONGER THAN FAITH?

Why was it so important for the Israelites to *act?* I believe that this situation finds its parallel in our times. Many patients whom I encounter in the hospital have been told that they must undertake certain measures for the sake of their health—special diets, adequate sleep and exercise, abstaining from alcohol, taking proper doses of medication daily. Yet many of these people, whose return to health—a form of personal redemption—depends on such steps, only comply partially. Some don't comply at all.

But God's message seems to be, "You've got to act along with Me. If you want liberation, I'll go along 100 percent, but you have to give 100 percent as well." Most people fall very short of this ideal. They rely on miracles, instead of actively participating in their own well-being.

In Egypt, it was clear that the people had to act. The blood that they were to place on their doorposts would *not* be solely from the slaughtered lamb. According to the Midrash, that blood would be mixed with the blood of all the circumcisions that took place that night for the purpose of permitting individuals to participate in the ritual of the lamb. So the Israelites had to take two steps on the night they were to leave Egypt: slaughtering the paschal lamb and circumcising those males who had not yet undergone it.

These acts presented an opportunity for Moses to resolve his crisis of faith. Remember that the episode began with Moses's *not* performing the ritual circumcision for his second son, because he had just learned that innocent Egyptian firstborn would be slain, a punishment that he initially found unfathomable. But having weathered that crisis and witnessed the pharaoh's responses to each of the earlier plagues, Moses had gained new understanding and perspective. He also realized that human beings had to take steps to achieve redemption. Moreover, only by undertaking common positive actions would the Israelites become a unified people.

When the people placed blood on their doorposts, God declared, in effect, "I will not allow destruction to enter into that home." On this "night of watching," the people *merited* protection because they had taken action. Nowadays, the obvious parallel is the placing of the *mezuzah,* the religious symbol containing the *Sh'ma,* the Jewish declaration of faith—"Hear, O Israel, the Eternal, our God, the Eternal is one"—on doorposts. This is a statement of Jewish identity. Notice that many people also place *mezuzot inside* the house, rather than just on the entry door. Just like the blood sign in Egypt, the *mezuzah* is a sign "to you." As each person enters a house and proceeds from room to room, he or she always sees a *mezuzah*, a reminder to act properly and not bring destructive energy into that home.

Showing an external sign of your heritage on the outside of your home is equally important. It publicly declares who you are. Only by making such a statement can you truly be liberated. The only way to gain respect from others is by respecting yourself. As Shakespeare reminded us in *Hamlet*, "This above all: to thine own self be true."

So positive actions are vital. That is why the late Viktor Frankl, the noted psychiatrist, and other prominent people have suggested that we need *two* statues along the coasts of the United States. On the East Coast, we already have the Statue of Liberty. This reminds us of our rights. But on the West Coast—to provide necessary balance—a Statue of Responsibility is needed. This would remind us that what we *do* reflects how we choose to live our lives. We need to be active partners with God in carrying out His work.

There are a number of other interesting aspects to the night of the Exodus from Egypt. The people are told to eat the sacrificial lamb "in haste." That is a little hard to understand. After all, the Israelites have been enslaved in Egypt for 210 years. After this protracted wait for salvation, and with redemption near, they should be ready. Why should they eat in haste? I believe that this description represents how redemption actually comes. Each of us may pray and plan for deliverance, but when it actually happens, we are invariably caught off guard. We are not ready.

I observe this reality quite frequently at my medical center. For example, last year, when a ninety-four-year-old man was hospitalized, I had the opportunity to meet his children, who were in their fifties and sixties. They desperately wanted to talk about deep, existential issues with him, such as illness, mortality, and fear of death. They had always delayed talking about these subjects.

But during his hospitalization, they were afraid that the right time had not yet arrived to discuss such matters. Their father was soon moved to the intensive care unit, where a tube inserted into his mouth made it impossible for him to speak. *That* was when the family really needed to talk to him, but it was too late. Witnessing this development, I was reminded how we are frequently unprepared for the most important moments in our lives, just like the Israelites in Egypt.

I recognize that it is human nature not to want to discuss such frightening issues. Some people are so afraid of illness and death that they go to great lengths to remove themselves from any reminders of it. An oncologist once told me that people often do not want to sit next to him at parties. They are afraid that if they see him socially, they may end up seeing him professionally—as his patients. That same attitude makes people afraid to talk about many critically important things; they worry that if they so much as mention their fears, these will actually come to pass.

As difficult as it is to talk about such issues as cancer, mortality, or funeral arrangements, it is certainly possible to do so. I have found that often, when a son or daughter spends some time with a parent in a pleasant setting, such as taking a walk through a garden, great communication is possible. I hope that many families will share the profound experience of relating to each other in just such a way, for it can help bring liberation and redemption to everyone involved.

When does redemption come? We learn that the Israelites were delivered from Egypt at midnight, in the middle of pitch-black darkness. At a time like that, people are usually frightened. So from the story of the Israelites, we can see that redemption does not come when things are going well. Rather, it occurs at moments of agony, darkness, and fright. As a popular saying reminds us, "It is always darkest before the dawn."

This message is universal, just as the creation of the Israelite nation certainly has universal implications. All who want to join in God's mission are welcomed, as long as they share the commitment to make the world a better place. But as we have seen, words and statements of belief are not enough. These individuals need to demonstrate their willingness through their *actions;* by living according to certain moral and ethical standards, as well as by undergoing certain rituals, such as male circumcision.

As the Israelites prepared to depart from Egypt, they packed their most precious possessions, including the gifts that the Egyptians had given them—jewels of silver and gold, and fancy garments. But Moses carried something special, something of even greater value. What he took with him would let him lead the people on their long journey to the Promised Land.

CHAPTER 15

The Bones of Joseph

M OSES REALIZED that he needed something that would give him and his people the strength to proceed through unknown territory on a very long journey. Even though the most direct route to Canaan took only eleven days on foot, the Israelites' wanderings and travels would take much longer.

God did not let the Israelites proceed along the shortest, easiest route. He knew their nature: their slave mentality, fears, and dependence on others for sustenance. So "God led them not by the way of the land of the Philistines, although that was near; for God said: 'Lest the people regret when they see war, and they return to Egypt.'"

Of course, God was right. Throughout their travels, the Israelites could not cope with many challenges or confrontations with others. Time after time, they regretted having even left Egypt. They seemed to forget, almost immediately, just how hard life had been there. Soon, all they could think about was the security that came with being slaves—particularly, the confidence of knowing where their next meal would come from. It seemed to be far easier to take the Israelites out of Egypt than to take Egypt out of the Israelites. At one point, the Israelites started craving the foods they ate while they were slaves: "We remember the fish, which we ate in Egypt for nothing; the cucumbers and the melons, and the leeks, and the onions and the garlic."

It is a human tendency to embellish memories of past events. This is as true today as it was with the Israelites. Psychologists refer to this phenomenon as "healing fiction," but the process remains the same as it has always been. We create and recreate our memories based on our states of mind at any particular time. Another thing that is as true today as it was then is that the long road, which is the road less traveled, is usually the one that gets us where we want to go. There are never any shortcuts to the Promised Land.

The long journey of life is a climb, a hard zigzag up a mountain. It is also like climbing a tall ladder. Progress is measured as we ascend from each rung to the next. We achieve peace of mind only by regarding each of those steps as a major accomplishment.

The journey of the Israelites can inspire us as we take the long route to where we want to go. And the story of the Exodus can provide us with some tips on what to "pack" for such a trip.

FORGIVENESS BRINGS REDEMPTION

What did Moses carry with him on the long, difficult journey out of Egypt? He took the bones of Joseph, in accordance with the oath that Joseph made the Israelites swear many years earlier, right before his death: "God will surely remember you, and you shall carry up my bones from here."

That deathbed conversation was very powerful. Everyone involved in a deathbed ritual senses the depth, the mystery, and the holiness of such a moment, realizing that the words exchanged should not be taken lightly. Often, parents use such an occasion for a particular purpose. Frequently, a dying father or mother asks the children to care for the surviving parent after he or she is gone.

But sometimes, such oaths of obligation create much inner struggle and stress for the children involved. One of my clients, Linda, was asked by her father shortly before his death, "Will you take care of Mom after I'm gone?" She immediately responded, "Yes, Daddy, of course I will," and this is what she has done. But this process has not been easy for her. On the contrary, it has dredged up all kinds of painful childhood memories, including her mother's abusive behavior toward her and her siblings. So Linda finds herself in a quandary. Although she intends to keep honoring that commitment, she struggles as she fulfills her promise each day.

Moses, however, had no difficulty fulfilling Joseph's final request. As he carried Joseph's bones, he recognized that he now had more than just his staff with which to lead the people. That rod symbolized empowerment, while the bones of Joseph, which were carried in an ark, were the source of his spiritual strength.

As the Israelites looked at Joseph's ark, I imagine they thought of his life and his values. They recalled that he epitomized forgiveness and reconciliation. After all, he forgave his brothers for all that they did to him: attempted murder, kidnapping, and selling him into slavery.

Joseph transcended all the difficulties he experienced in Egypt by recognizing the Divine providence that brought him there. He came to understand that he was not just an individual, but that a higher purpose guided him. He ultimately discovered that he had been brought to Egypt to save many lives during a severe famine. Most importantly, he was able to save his own family and people from certain starvation.

So the bones of Joseph reminded the Israelites that on the long journey ahead, all kinds of family issues and conflicts would undoubtedly arise. But all of these could be resolved—peacefully— by adopting the attitude and faith demonstrated by Joseph. Forgiveness is the way to get to the Promised Land. Ingesting the psychic toxicity of others only prevents a person from getting on with his or her life.

One of my clients, Marianne, had not spoken with her brothers for years after they had argued over their family business. But Marianne finally felt that this rancor had gone on long enough. Life was too short to dwell on old wounds. So she called up her brothers and said to each of them, "Let's get together for Thanksgiving at my house. We'll do it in memory of Mom. Mom would have wanted it that way." The family did get together. They still have a long road to travel before they completely trust and understand each other, but at least they are speaking to each other and keeping channels of communication open.

Joseph is a great role model for learning about such forgiveness. I doubt that anything brothers and sisters do to each other today can even approach the gravity of the offenses that Joseph's brothers committed against him. Yet he was able to forgive them.

So the presence of Joseph's bones in the midst of the people was very important, indeed. They were a constant reminder to the people about how to live a holy life, since his life was the embodiment of moral law. An interesting Midrash makes this point very clearly. It reminds us that a few weeks after the Israelites left Egypt, they arrived at Mount Sinai, where they received the Ten Commandments and the rest of the law. The tablets containing the teachings and laws were placed in an ark that the people carried with them throughout their travels.

So the people actually carried *two* arks—one containing the bones of Joseph, and one holding the Ten Commandments. The Midrash tells us that the surrounding nations wondered why the children of Israel carried these two similar arks and why they treated them in the same reverential manner. They concluded that "He [Joseph] whose remains are preserved in the one ark loyally obeyed the Divine commands enshrined in the other."

As the Israelites wandered through the desert, they thought about many aspects of Joseph's life. They recalled that it was because of him that their ancestors had originally come to Egypt. But they also remembered that Joseph rose from servitude to become the highest member of the royal court, second only to the pharaoh. So the people knew that they were not just liberated slaves, but the descendants of a prince! That knowledge should have given them some perspective about their worth as individuals who had not always been subservient to others.

Joseph's coffin also added a deeper perspective to the people's daily lives. Being in the presence of death reminded the Israelites of their own mortality and inspired them to introspection and self-evaluation. It is important for each of us to have a healthy acknowledgment of mortality, for it leads us to make different kinds of decisions than we would if we believed that we could live forever. Being able to perceive that different matters have varying degrees of importance helps us prioritize our actions and values. Many physicians I work with are not easily perturbed by some of the ordinary issues that trouble other people. They see these as mere inconveniences, in contrast to the real life-and-death struggles that they encounter daily.

Awareness of human mortality goes hand-in-hand with an even more important recognition: that even though Joseph had died, his spirit still guided the people. One of the great lessons that Joseph bestowed in this way was his message of hope. After all, years before he had said, "God will surely remember you, and you shall carry up my bones from here." He recognized that even if he could not make the journey in his lifetime, he would eventually get to the Promised Land along with his people. Not only that, but his remains were ultimately buried in Shechem (Nablus), where they remain to this day.

FINDING HOLINESS EVEN IN DARKNESS

Sometimes we can achieve our goals during our lifetime; in other instances, it is left for our descendants to fulfill our dreams. Whether we are present physically—or in spirit—we can, and will, still share in these achievements. I often remind my students that *the goal is really the journey itself.*

Recently, I ran into a wonderful man who volunteers at the medical center where I work. He told me that he had become interested in exploring the Judaism that he had abandoned as a youth in Europe. He did not recall how to perform many of the rituals, but he told me that he had just purchased a *mezuzah* to put on the doorpost of his home. "Rabbi," he said, "I know I'm not religious yet." "But you already are," I replied. I wanted him to recognize that he has already begun the journey, which is, in fact, the goal.

This process is what the Rev. Martin Luther King Jr. expressed so well in Memphis as he addressed sanitation workers on April 3, 1968, the night before his assassination. Drawing upon the story of the Exodus from Egypt to describe the journey of African Americans to true freedom, he said, "And I've looked over and I've seen the promised land. I may not get there with you, but I want you to know tonight that we, as a people, will get to the promised land." Those words had a powerful impact on the people present, and they continue to move us today.

The voices of the past are very important. One patient told me, "Every day, I hear the voices of my deceased father and grandfather." Although our patriarchs and matriarchs may be long gone, they too are still with us. As one of my students observed, "I feel as if Abraham, Sarah, Isaac, Jacob, Joseph, and the rest of them are part of my family." Of course, he was correct—they are.

Consequently, many Jews do not regard burial plots outside of Israel as their relatives' final resting places. Like Joseph, many people have been reinterred in Israel. In his will, for instance, Theodor Herzl (1860–1904), the father of modern Zionism, asked to be buried in his family's plot in Vienna until the Jewish people would transfer his remains to Israel. And in August 1949, shortly after the state of Israel was established, Herzl's dream came true. His remains were brought to the new state and reinterred on Mount Herzl in Jerusalem.

The people participating in the Exodus had their own dreams

and expectations, but they needed constant reassurance. So they were given special protection and guidance: "And the Lord went before them by day in a pillar of cloud, to lead them on the way; and by night in a pillar of fire, to give them light; that they might go by day and by night; the pillar of cloud by day, and the pillar of fire by night, departed not from before the people."

These manifestations supplemented the natural illuminations of the sun and the moon, and represented the continuous Divine Presence watching over the people. The cloud and the fire were actually one entity. What appeared to be a cloud during the day appeared as fire at night. From this phenomenon, we can see that something ordinary—like a cloud—can be invested with a special quality. Thus, instead of bemoaning a cloudy day, waiting for the sun to appear, we can find value and meaning in the clouds themselves. This perspective can help us find enchantment in everyday objects and occurrences, as we learn to appreciate each moment of each day as something holy and precious. The Israelites had the opportunity to experience the extraordinary in the ordinary, as well as the truly miraculous, as they neared the Sea of Reeds.

CHAPTER 16

Crossing the Sea

A S THE PEOPLE APPROACHED the Sea of Reeds, followed
closely by the pursuing Egyptians, the sea miraculously
parted, allowing them to cross on dry ground. Then the returning waters drowned the pursuing Egyptian soldiers and their
chariots and horses. At this point, we are told that the people "believed in the Lord, and in His servant Moses."

This wholehearted response of the people is a very powerful
statement, particularly when we remember how they responded
at the beginning of this journey.

But now, they have not only observed miraculous events, they
have participated in them. So the *experience* that the people have
undergone has changed them. Their belief has now become an
integral part of their selves. I am reminded that when he was
asked, "Do you believe in God?" C. G. Jung, the great disciple of
Sigmund Freud, responded, "I don't believe. I *know*." Similarly,
Clarissa Pinkola Estes, in her book *Women Who Run with the
Wolves*, distinguishes between knowledge of the head (cerebral
knowledge), heart (emotional knowledge), and ovaries (instinc-
tual knowledge). At the Sea of Reeds, Israelite knowledge ex-
panded to encompass all of the above.

To better understand this new stage in the Israelites' religious development, we need to look at what happened before the people arrived at the Sea of Reeds, as well as what occurred there. The tenth plague—the killing of the firstborn—had affected every Egyptian household. In the middle of that plague, the pharaoh actually ordered the Israelites out of his country. By the time the Israelites came to the Sea of Reeds, they had already been out of Egypt for three days.

God instructed Moses to tell the Israelites to "turn back" and encamp by the sea. It seems strange that the people should be told to go *back* if they were in the process of going *out* of the land. However, I believe that this order was given to test the pharaoh's response after the slaves' departure.

When the pharaoh saw that the Israelites had turned back, he gleefully noted that "the wilderness has shut them in," and he planned to attack them. This gives us a glimpse of the pharaoh's true personality. Nothing that happened to him had any effect on him. There was no way to get through to him. Even after the deaths of all those innocent Egyptian children, including his own son, he had not changed. He had a heart of stone.

I have watched people respond this way. It is as if aspects of themselves are unresponsive to any therapeutic intervention. A portion of their hearts is made out of stone.

Let me tell you about one such person, a dentist, who seems unresponsive to any outside intervention. Married and with two children, he seems to have everything going right for him, yet he is full of rage and frustration. It is impossible for him to open up to anyone, even those closest to him. When he perceives remarks as confrontational, he does not respond, but retreats into himself. While introversion is certainly not abnormal, when carried to this sort of extreme, it becomes pathological.

The consequences of his behavior are readily apparent. Despite his technical brilliance as a dentist, his private practice has not been successful. Patients interpret his icy demeanor as callousness. Since his own practice has dwindled, he recently joined a large group practice, where he will not have to worry about ongoing relationships with patients.

On a personal level as well, he suffers from the stoniness of his heart. He cannot function well in most gatherings because of his lack of social graces, so his wife does not wish to go places with him. His loneliness and inability to communicate with others have created a vicious circle from which he cannot extricate himself.

That same stubbornness characterized *all* of the pharaoh's actions. As is true for most people who thrive on controlling others, the pharaoh needed his slaves. They were part of his self-definition. He was lost without them. The Israelites felt a need for him as well. They still saw themselves as slaves who had at least been provided for while they were in Egypt. Maybe they suffered, but at least they would not have found themselves in front of a deep sea with no way to cross.

So that is the scene—the Israelites were trapped between the pharaoh's army and the Sea of Reeds. They felt hopeless and lost, and began to cry out in prayer. God responded that this was not a time to cry, but *to act*. He told Moses, "Why do you cry unto Me? Speak unto the children of Israel, that they go forward" into the sea.

I certainly believe in prayer, but there is a time for everything, as we read in Ecclesiastes, and in a situation like this, action was needed first. Prayer could follow.

I am reminded of a fundamentalist religious couple whose child was a patient of mine a few years ago. They had deferred treatment for their child, believing that their prayers alone would heal her. But their dedicated pastor kept explaining to them that the task of healing could best be accomplished by a team of trained physicians, a loving family, and God. He convinced them to let the child undergo the tests and therapy the doctors had recommended, while keeping up their faith and their prayers. In the end, their prayers were answered. Their daughter was cured.

CREATING NEW WORLDS IS OUR TASK

So our actions are critical. Faith is fine, but it usually requires action to be sustained. As a matter of fact, when the Israelites came to the Sea of Reeds, despite all the miracles they had already witnessed, they were reluctant to rely on God's promise to part the waters for them. At first, none of them was willing to take that first step into the sea, a step that required, literally, a leap of faith.

My daughter Chana told me a story that describes the dynamics of this situation. It seems that a great tightrope walker had strung a wire between two high mountain peaks and announced that he would walk across this chasm the next day at two o'clock in the afternoon. All the local townspeople showed up and watched breathlessly as the man set out and slowly, painstakingly, accomplished this awesome feat. They applauded. And then he announced that he would perform an even greater feat the next day at the same time.

At the appointed hour, the performer appeared again. Since word of his deed on the previous day had spread, the crowd was even larger. This time, the tightrope walker showed the crowd a small unicycle and announced that he would ride it from one peak to the other and then back. And he did! The crowd went wild.

The next day, the man repeated this amazing feat. And the next. But each day, he modified his task somewhat, making it even more difficult and more challenging. One day, he juggled balls as he rode across; the next, he rode the cycle backwards; and the next, he performed blindfolded. The crowds kept growing in size and enthusiasm. Finally, on the tenth day, the performer said, "I need one volunteer to help me out this time." No one moved; no one raised a hand; no one spoke up. Cheers, words, and platitudes are great, but they mean nothing unless accompanied by action.

In a song from *My Fair Lady* aptly entitled "Show Me," Eliza Doolittle sings:

Words, words, words
I'm so sick of words.
I get words all day through
First from him, now from you . . .

Many people have shared similar feelings with me, particularly people who have spoken to me candidly after suffering a death in their family. During their moments of greatest need—right after the funeral—friends and relatives said, "Please let me know if there is anything I can do." Most of these well-meaning people did not have any further contact with the bereaved. They felt that they had done their duty by showing up and saying the appropriate words. They did not really want to be bothered any more.

This attitude also prevails in the business world. A young computer analyst I know has been repeatedly commended by his superiors for outstanding performance, and he is waiting patiently for their words to be reflected in a salary increase or a bonus. But his managers have been reluctant to bring up his case with the company directors because they want to demonstrate how well they work within tight budgetary constraints. So their words have proven to be empty and meaningless, just like the cheers of the people who were at that mountain with the tightrope walker.

The people cheering that performer remind me of the scene that unfolded at the Sea of Reeds. Some two or three million Israelites stood at the shore of the sea. They had seen many miracles in Egypt, and were promised another one now—the splitting of the sea. Even while they had camped near the sea, another wonder had taken place. The pillar of cloud that had guided them by day did not disappear at night into a pillar of fire, as it usually did. Instead, the cloud stayed behind them, bringing darkness to the pursuing Egyptians and thus offering the Israelites an extra measure of protection.

Yet, the Midrash tells us that when the moment of truth arrived—the time to go forward into the sea—none of them budged!

Finally, a man named Nahshon ben Amminadab demonstrated his absolute faith by jumping into the raging waters. As everyone else watched, the waters continued to swirl around him, finally reaching as high as his nostrils. Then, they began to recede. At that point, the sea began to part, allowing Nahshon and all the others to cross over. The Egyptians pursued the Israelites into the sea.

Then, God commanded Moses to stretch forth his hand over the sea. With that, the waters crashed down on the Egyptians, drowning all of them. Events had now come full circle. Years earlier, when the pharaoh first enslaved the Israelites, he worried about their potential power. So he decreed that all their male children should die, saying: "Every son that is born you shall cast into the river." Now the Egyptian males were drowned as they pursued the Israelites into the sea.

God responded more than once in a way designed to teach the pharaoh about the limits of human power. The pharaoh had wanted to kill the Israelites—called God's "firstborn"—but he was not successful. As the pharaoh stood by helplessly, all the Egyptian firstborn sons were killed during the tenth plague. At the Sea of Reeds, even more Egyptians perished.

There are echoes of other biblical events here. After the great flood, God made a covenant—symbolized by a rainbow—to never again destroy the entire world by floodwater. The covenant was kept, but God could still bring death and destruction to a nation —the Egyptians—if it might create a better world for the rest of humanity.

So the Egyptian soldiers drowning in the Sea of Reeds brought about the immediate liberation of the Israelites, who finally expressed their complete belief in God and in Moses. Why did this episode affect their belief systems so intensely, unlike previous occurrences? Of course, in this case, the people felt the personal salvation of escaping with their lives and being victorious over the Egyptians, but I think that something deeper was at work.

I believe that the profound experience of the Israelites was actually taking part in a new type of creation. What went on at this splitting of the sea was a new manifestation of what had taken place at the very beginning of the world. Remember what happened on the third day of creation: "God said: 'Let the waters under the heaven be gathered together unto one place, and let the dry land appear.' And it was so."

Just as God separated the waters at the beginning of time, thereby creating a new continent, so now God did the same thing, creating a new area of dry land in the midst of the sea: "And the waters were divided. And the children of Israel went into the midst of the sea upon the dry ground." Now, through their actions, the Israelites became partners in this new creation.

During the first creation, God acted alone in separating the waters. But this time, as shown in the story of Nahshon, the first Israelite to go into the Sea of Reeds, God indicated that creation will not happen without the help of humanity. We are to be partners with God in creating together. As Henry David Thoreau wrote in his poem "Nature":

> Some still work give me to do,—
> Only—be it near to you!

Now we can understand why the experiential knowledge gained by the Israelites was so powerful. They *participated* in creating a new world. That remains our mandate as well. We are to be active participants in the continuing process of birthing and rebirthing that characterizes our lives, both as individuals and as members of a greater community. We are to work at changing unhealthy patterns of behavior in our own lives and in the society around us. We are to build bridges of understanding between individuals and between peoples. Only by helping to create a better world will we bring about redemption for ourselves and the rest of humanity. Only then will we be able to lift our voices in a song of heartfelt thanks and praise to God.

CHAPTER 17

The Song at the Sea

AFTER THE PEOPLE CROSSED the Sea of Reeds that had miraculously parted for them, they joined Moses in a beautiful song of praise to God. I find these verses to be among the most uplifting and meaningful in the Bible, yet some aspects of this song are truly surprising.

First of all, I am amazed at Moses's sudden ability to sing. After all, Moses initially described himself as being "not a man of words . . . for I have heaviness of speech, and heaviness of tongue." Remember that he even needed his brother Aaron to serve as his spokesman. Yet, after leaving Egypt, he was suddenly able to sing. Apparently, this liberating experience had transformed him.

Secondly, in the past, Moses and the Israelites had often operated on parallel but separate tracks. They had rarely acted together, and when they did, the results were not always positive. But now, the wonders that freedom brought enabled Moses and the people to join forces and act and sing in unison and harmony. As they sang together, they demonstrated unity, not the disharmony that they had sometimes shown in the past.

These poetic verses praise God. Moses and the people sang

these words in a novel way—responsively. Moses recited one phrase, and the people responded with the next. Several times, the people repeated a familiar refrain as a chorus to emphasize an important idea. They sang with one mind and one heart.

In the Bible, the song is introduced with a simple phrase that is difficult to translate from the original Hebrew. Most often, it is translated as, "Then sang Moses and the children of Israel this song unto the Lord." But that is not accurate. Instead of the past tense—"sang"—the text actually uses the future tense, so that the verse really reads, "Then Moses will sing."

The Midrash explains that everyone who recites this song in this world will merit the opportunity to recite it in the world to come. Most people I meet think of that world as existing at some far-off future time—the end of days. But the world to come—eternity—exists *right now!* Being able to recognize it just requires that we adjust how we look at the world.

In the physical world, we are bound by time and other limitations. I find it sad that so many people spend their time reminiscing about the past or anticipating the future, rather than focusing on each precious, unique moment of the here-and-now.

I think of two German brothers I know. They come from Berlin, where for years they and their families were cut off from each other by the ugly wall that divided that city. But finally, with the collapse of communism and the dismantling of the wall, the brothers were joyfully reunited. At first they were elated, particularly when they both emigrated to the United States. But I have noticed that they have not been able to enjoy their new freedom and higher standard of living. Understandably, they have a lot of bitter memories about the past, which they never tire of retelling. They have genuine worries about saving enough money to guarantee them and their children a brighter future. So despite their physical freedom, they find themselves prisoners of their past and future, unable to enjoy their new lives in America.

I understand how such concerns and fears can keep us all from being content, how they can keep us chained to concepts of time. But if we progress to a higher level of spiritual understanding, we can actually experience timelessness—eternity—even during this difficult earthly existence. It is possible to live each momentary experience as part of eternity. William Blake described this process succinctly in his poem, "Auguries of Innocence":

> To see a World in a Grain of Sand,
> And a Heaven in a Wild Flower,
> Hold Infinity in the palm of your hand,
> And Eternity in an hour.

MIRACLES SURROUND US

Each of us has the capacity to live life in this manner, to experience moments that go beyond our ego, and be transported to a higher, transpersonal level. At such times, past, present, and future become one. Being in the here-and-now can help us get to that lofty plane and transcend time.

Moses and the children of Israel achieved this experience through their heartfelt singing, and song remains one way to reach this higher state. A song is a very powerful thing. In fact, the entire Torah is referred to as a song: "Now therefore write this song for yourselves, and teach it to the children of Israel; put it in their mouths." Like poetry, Torah touches our soul, our emotional core, rather than just our analytical minds. Other creative processes such as art, dance, meditation, and prayer can also help us get in touch with our Higher Self.

However, what the Israelites witnessed and felt when they crossed the Sea of Reeds was very special indeed. The Midrash points out that the lowliest maidservant who crossed the sea saw things that even the greatest prophets of later times never perceived. That was because even the most humble people *recognized* the divinity in what they saw. They were so elevated and so moved that they proclaimed as one, "This is my God, and I will glorify Him." They understood the miracle they experienced.

Miracles still take place in our day and age, but people do not always recognize them. As a matter of fact, they usually tend to explain them away as purely scientific events, mass hallucinations, or whatever else might make such things rationally plausible. But a "miracle" is not so much what we see, but how we see it.

I know a lovely young couple, Nick and Marilyn, who were childless for the first thirteen years of their marriage. They underwent numerous evaluations, tests, and procedures, all to no avail. Fertility consultants provided some encouragement to them, but as the years went by, they became less and less hopeful that they would biologically have a child of their own.

One day, in desperation, Marilyn's sister decided that she would start a prayer campaign on behalf of the couple. On a particular day—March 15—she sat down and wrote or faxed messages to relatives and friends around the world, asking them to pray for Marilyn and Nick. Soon prayers were being recited around the globe for these young people.

A few months later, Marilyn suspected that she was pregnant. In disbelief, she went to her obstetrician, who confirmed the happy news. The doctor also supplied some important information. The baby was due to be born the following March 15—one year to the day from the date the prayer campaign had begun.

I wish that all of our prayers could be answered so positively and so quickly. But, like all mortals, I am limited in what I can understand about Divine providence.

Even in the case of ordinary, nonmiraculous happenings, our perceptions are influenced by what we know, or what we think we know. Sid, a medical resident at Cedars-Sinai Medical Center in Los Angeles, told me a story that confirms this point. During one of his early pediatric rotations, he examined a child who had been diagnosed with an unusual syndrome. As Sid noted some of the symptoms, he said to his supervising physician, "I've never seen anything like this before." The supervisor responded, "Oh yes, you have. You just didn't recognize it." That is so true of many of our life experiences. If we are not attuned to the greater meaning of an event or encounter, we may not recognize it even when we have the opportunity to do so.

HOPE CONQUERS DESPAIR

As the Israelites neared the end of their song, they proclaimed the final, powerful phrase: "The Lord will reign for ever and ever." It is no wonder that these words are familiar to so many people of various faiths. They represent the main purpose of the liberation that they celebrate: to develop a kingdom of God here on earth. Life is a continual process of creation and re-creation. We are partners with God in creating a better world for all people. That is our mission and our purpose.

It is the same for each of us—young and old, man and woman. And it is a woman—Miriam—who played a pivotal role during the song at the sea. We read: "And Miriam the prophetess, the sister of Aaron, took a timbrel in her hand; and all the women went out after her with timbrels and with dances. And Miriam sang unto them." Miriam inspired the women to follow her and join her in song.

But the Bible refers to her in a rather unusual way. She is called "the prophetess, the sister of Aaron." There is no mention of her relationship to Moses. This description leaps out at us, begging for clarification. In my view, this phrase is inextricably linked with something that happened before Moses was born. At that time, when Miriam was the sister of Aaron only, she had a prophetic vision which foretold the birth of Moses and the liberation of an entire people.

Moses's parents—Amram and Yocheved—were at first afraid to bring another child into the world, since the pharaoh had ordered that all newborn Hebrew males be killed. So according to the Midrash, Amram and Yocheved separated for three years. But then, Miriam told them about her prophetic vision: a son would be born to them who would save the Israelites from the Egyptians. Only then did Amram return to his wife. Soon afterwards, Moses was conceived.

So Miriam had every right to sing and express her joy with great fervor. She knew that salvation would come, that something good would happen, even when everyone around her was in despair. As she sang, the Midrash tells us she was reminding herself and everyone around her: "Remember the prophecy from my youth. We had to wait, but I knew that a leader would come along to save us. I was Aaron's sister then, but I predicted that Moses would be born and that this joyful day would finally come. I had hope while those around me were despondent."

Miriam's song contains yet another message. When you have strong, intuitive feelings about something you believe in, do not let yourself be overwhelmed by the negative voices and despair of others. People may try to drown out your message of hope because they are afraid of change, which is uncomfortable for them to contemplate. But pursue your dream, especially when it involves working as a partner with God. By doing so, you will help bring about the kingdom of God in your life.

As the Israelites journeyed further into the wilderness, they would actively participate in this great endeavor. Soon they would stand at the base of Mount Sinai and receive the Ten Commandments, which would be given to them to transmit to all the other people on earth.

PART III

The Challenge of Faith

CHAPTER 18

Spiritual Thirst

I T WOULD TAKE SEVEN WEEKS for the people to travel from Egypt to Mount Sinai.

The journey was not easy. For three days after crossing the Sea of Reeds, the Israelites had no water to drink. This seems ironic, since they had just passed through the sea. Their predicament reminds me of *The Rime of the Ancient Mariner*, by Samuel Taylor Coleridge:

> Water, water, everywhere,
> Nor any drop to drink.

When they reached a place called Marah, meaning "bitter," and discovered that the water there was also undrinkable, the Israelites began to complain to Moses.

Their anger was understandable. After all, the first plague that they had witnessed in Egypt transformed the waters of the Nile into blood. Perhaps the people worried that the bitter waters of Marah were the beginning of a new plague. They quickly went from singing praises to God to expressing fear, confusion, and bewilderment.

Yet Moses did not berate or yell at the people. Instead, he asked God for guidance and direction.

God showed Moses a nearby tree, which Moses cast into the waters, rendering them sweet. The Midrash understands this incident as indicating that the people might have been demonstrating a *spiritual* as well as a physical thirst. This interpretation recognizes that water often appears as a symbol for the Torah and its teachings, as well as for the unconscious. At this point—before the people arrived at Mount Sinai—the Torah had not yet been revealed. So for three days, they searched for "water"—something meaningful to sustain them on their journey.

Right after Moses sweetened the water for them, God "made for them a statute and an ordinance." That is, God revealed to them several core laws for living. These included the commandment to honor one's father and mother, and the laws of civil jurisprudence. These laws showed the people how to get along with each other in familial and societal settings, and temporarily abated their physical and spiritual thirst.

The whole episode at Marah remains difficult to understand. Perhaps it serves to remind us about the importance of finding a meaningful purpose in our lives. The significant part of any journey is not the goal—the end—but rather, the *process* of getting there. I sometimes remind my children that our trips to Yosemite do not begin when we arrive at that beautiful park; they commence as soon as we leave our home and get in the car.

For any trip to be worthwhile, it needs to be meaningful and directed. Psychiatrist Irving Yalom wrote that a person achieves mental health when he or she is genuinely involved in some meaningful activity. For the Israelites, that activity meant being engaged in and loving the teachings of the Torah. This would provide them with a spiritual path to a more transcendent life, one that is lived beyond the humdrum aspects of everyday existence.

At Marah, God further educated and reassured the people, allaying their fears that they might be subjected to the sort of plagues they had witnessed in Egypt. God told them that if they would keep the Divine commandments, "I will put none of the diseases upon you which I have put upon the Egyptians; for I am the Lord Who heals you."

Physicians and other healers are certainly given great respect and recognition in Judaic tradition, which customarily bestows on them the honorary title of "our revered teachers." There is always the recognition that they are partners with God, privileged to have the training and opportunity to participate in the healing process.

One of my hospital volunteers, Isaac, a truly pious man, described his own understanding of this concept. Shortly before he was to undergo surgery, his internist introduced him to the surgeon who would perform the operation. After Isaac and the surgeon spoke for a while, Isaac said, "I have tremendous confidence in your *partner*." The confused surgeon responded, "But I have no partner. I'm in private practice." Yet Isaac repeated, "I have tremendous confidence in your partner," then gestured upward with his hand. Now the surgeon understood what he meant.

I wish that all physicians understood that the Hebrew word used to describe God as a "healer" connotes much more than just making a person better. It includes the concepts of tenderness and softness, qualities that all of us can emulate to become better healers.

FAITH IS DIFFICULT TO SUSTAIN

After reassuring the people that they would not suffer plagues, God led them to a place called Elim, where there were twelve springs and many palm trees. They encamped there by the waters for a few days, then resumed their journey. But they quickly demonstrated how fearful they were.

When they arrived at a place named Rephidim, where there was no water to drink, the Israelites again started complaining. Rather than responding compassionately as he had at Marah, Moses reacted very angrily: "Why do you strive with me? Why do you try the Lord?" He cried out to God, but this time, he did not sound like a leader: "What shall I do unto this people? They are almost ready to stone me."

At Marah, Moses had "kept his cool." But now, he seemed to have lost it. He was demonstrating his human fears and frailty, worrying about his own physical safety in the presence of what could be an ugly mob. God told Moses to walk among the people. By mingling with them, Moses could see that they were not about to stone him.

God was giving Moses another lesson, a more important one. In effect, God was telling him, "Look at these people. The only reason that you are a leader is because of them. They are just human. Do not be so hard on them." Then God instructed Moses to take his stick and hit a rock with it. Moses complied and abundant water flowed from the rock.

Then the people asked a most amazing question: "Is the Lord among us, or not?" They had been rescued from Egypt, led through the Sea of Reeds, protected by Divine clouds of glory, had their water sweetened and miraculously supplied for them, and yet they still asked this fundamental question!

Their lack of faith is difficult to comprehend. The Midrash suggests that the problem was the people's attitude. Even while complaining of thirst, the people might actually have had some water with them, but their supply was inadequate—or at least, it *seemed* so to them. That type of concern remains a central issue for us. What is "enough"? When do we have enough? Sadly, for many people the answer to that last question is "never." The Israelites actually preferred the routine and security of slavery to the risks of being free. In Egypt, they could at least be certain of being fed every day. But as free people, they were responsible for locating and retrieving their own water. So from time to time, when things looked bad, they talked of returning to Egypt.

In recent years, I have come across similar cases of people who find freedom to be both a blessing and a challenge. A number of Iranian and Russian immigrants who have settled in Los Angeles have told me about their fears for their future. One middle-aged man said, "When I came to this great country, all I could think about was the freedom here. But then I had to retrain, studying all over again, and working my way up from the bottom. I also had many problems with the language. It has been worthwhile for my family, but it has been hard on all of us. Even though I know it seems crazy, sometimes I think we should have stayed where we were."

So it is not surprising that whenever the Israelites encountered difficulties, their thoughts quickly turned back to Egypt. But water wasn't the only deprivation they faced. A different kind of need would not only test their beliefs, but also teach them what faith was all about.

CHAPTER 19

Faith

OUT IN THE WILDERNESS where the Israelites found themselves, no crops were growing. No native vegetation could sustain them during their journey. So they began to worry about how they could possibly survive for even one day, let alone the period of time they would be in the desert.

Once again, they compared their present situation to their experience in Egypt. But their memories were highly selective. They did not seem to recall the beatings or the oppression. Rather, as soon as they felt their first hunger pangs, they complained to Moses and Aaron: "Would that we had died by the hand of the Lord in the land of Egypt, when we sat by the flesh-pots, when we did eat bread to the full; for *you* have brought us forth into this wilderness, to kill this whole assembly with hunger."

Note how quickly the people transformed Moses and Aaron from heroic liberators into villains. This behavior follows a common pattern. Whenever something goes wrong, it is natural to look for scapegoats. It's common for mothers or fathers to dote on a child who is doing well: "My child is so bright. My child is so accomplished." But when the same young person misbehaves, each parent may point to the other, saying, "Look what *your* kid has done now!"

In just this way, the Israelites turned on Moses and Aaron, who had freed them, but then brought them to an arid wilderness. The people were convinced that whatever they might have experienced in Egypt was better than a slow, torturous death by starvation.

Once again, God provided a miracle, telling Moses that "bread"—manna—would rain down daily from heaven upon the camp. The Midrash beautifully describes the significance of this miraculous event: "He Who created the day also created the sustenance for it." God did not just create the world and leave all the creatures on their own. Instead, God is actively concerned with providing them with what they need to sustain themselves.

Even the way that the manna was "packaged" is meaningful. The natural laws of creation were reversed to provide this wonderful food. The "bread" came *down* from heaven, rather than growing *up* from the earth. And before the manna descended, a layer of dew arose from the earth—rather than descending from the heavens—to protect it.

The manna may have been a miracle, but our ability to sustain ourselves daily is no less miraculous. The Israelites—and all of us now—could learn to recognize the Presence and involvement of God in every aspect of our everyday lives.

In order for the Israelites to learn this crucial lesson, they had to follow several simple rules regarding the manna. Every day, they would gather a certain amount of manna for each member of their household that would suffice for that day's needs. But they could not save any manna for the following day when, they were assured, more would be provided. They had to trust that the promise of God would be kept.

But they were not quite ready for that yet. Some of them stored away extra manna, but found that it bred worms. Moses was understandably angry with them and learned that it would take more than miracles to sustain their faith.

That becomes even clearer when we see what happens next. Moses told the Israelites that on Friday, the day before the Sabbath, they were to gather twice as much manna as usual, and they were *not* to go out on the Sabbath to look for manna. They had to save the extra manna for the Sabbath and it would not rot. Furthermore, no additional manna would fall from the heavens on the Sabbath. Despite these instructions, some people went out on the Sabbath to search for manna, which of course they did not find.

God seemed to be trying to drive home this message: "Do as I say. Trust Me. Don't worry. My Presence is with you and I will continue to provide for you." But it is very difficult for humans to absorb this reassuring lesson. I think of our situation today and wonder who—if anyone—never worries about what may happen tomorrow. As we approach the millennium, who really feels financially secure or enjoys complete job security? In these turbulent, volatile times, no one can predict the future of the stock market or the economy. We all recognize that whatever ups or downs ensue will be determined by forces beyond our control. That is quite a frightening prospect. So, no amount of manna—or money—is ever enough to provide us with security. The only real type of security that we can achieve is faith and trust in God.

LIVING IN THE HERE-AND-NOW
CAN EASE OUR ANXIETIES

As we have just seen, however, it is not so easy to acquire faith. It cannot be suddenly thrust upon us, even through manifestations of the Divine. But what can bring it about is a shift in perspective. The Israelites who tried to hoard extra manna demonstrated their lack of faith by focusing on their *future* needs, just as many of us, unfortunately, worry about our uncertain financial and other prospects.

The way to faith seems to involve living in the *present*—experiencing each moment—and not constantly worrying about what has been or what might be. Certainly, storing up reserves for the future is a prudent thing to do. However, having faith and trust in the here-and-now is paramount.

Observing the Sabbath by not working on that day is one way to demonstrate faith. This faith experience of the Sabbath can overflow into the rest of the week. But many people are not prepared to go that far. They calculate—quite rationally—that if they work a certain number of hours on the Sabbath, they will earn extra money and as a result, be more financially secure. But that is not the way the world operates. Steps A, B, and C do not necessarily lead to D. The future is always uncertain and unexpected.

Mikhail and Rosa, Russian immigrants who now live in Los Angeles, both worked on the Sabbath to earn extra money to get on their feet when they arrived in America. Then Mikhail, who was self-employed as an electrician, got hurt on the job and had to take time off. All the extra money he put aside was used up during his recuperation. As if that weren't enough, Rosa was involved in an accident while driving to work. Since her car was inadequately insured, she was forced to dip into her extra savings for the repairs.

Today, neither Mikhail nor Rosa works on the Sabbath. They are both happy, more relaxed, and grateful that they don't have to push so hard. Surprisingly, they have more money in the bank than ever. Mikhail landed several more lucrative jobs and they have prospered!

Many of the physicians I work with have also come to realize that their lives are not always directed by their well-laid plans. Over the past seven years or so, I have watched some of them modify their lifestyles and expectations. The growth of health maintenance organizations and other unforeseen aspects of managed care have greatly influenced their earning potential, causing them to reassess their needs and priorities.

None of us can rely solely on rational thinking and planning for the future. But by learning from the story of the manna, we can all take a leap of faith that can enable us to face each coming day with peace of mind. The fact that the manna was given on a daily basis is also instructive. After all, it could have been delivered in supplies guaranteed to last for several days at a time. But the Midrash teaches that God's daily ration of this food demonstrated Divine love for the Israelites. God took pleasure in providing them with sustenance on a daily basis, so that they could experience the Divine Presence every day.

When we have faith, we fully experience each moment of the here-and-now. We take the most mundane activity—such as eating—and elevate it. We savor each bite and taste each morsel of a chocolate-chip cookie, rather than gobbling it down. After eating a complete dinner, we acknowledge the source of our food by reciting the grace after meals.

By being aware of each moment, we reduce our anxiety about the future. We also deal better with many of the daily issues that cause us pain and distress. Problems with the basics of life, such as sex and food, often relate to not living in the moment. Some men have sexual fears related to performance anxiety. Such concerns are clear manifestations of worrying about the future, rather than focusing on the here-and-now. Similarly, some women struggle with complex eating disorders, such as anorexia or bulimia. They do not experience the pleasure of eating. Rather, they use food to soothe some inner conflict or pain.

Appreciating each moment requires a certain amount of retraining to look at the world in a different way. Much can be achieved through such a shift in perception. Many great works of poetry and art focus on capturing the beauty and uniqueness of a fleeting vision or emotion. In his poem, "Nature," Henry David Thoreau summarized how precious each glimpse of the natural world is to him:

> For I'd rather be thy child
> And pupil, in the forest wild,

Than be the king of men elsewhere,
And most sovereign slave of care;
To have one moment of thy dawn,
Than share the city's year forlorn.

Whether we find ourselves in a rural or an urban setting, living in the moment helps us lead healthier, less anxious lives. It also helps us achieve an even loftier goal. You may recall that, at the burning bush, God's name is given as *"Ehyeh,"* which means "I will always be with you." The essence of God is that the Divinity is with us at all times, a gift that we can indeed come to recognize.

The Israelites would learn more about how to follow the path of God as they proceeded toward Mount Sinai. But before they could continue their spiritual growth, they would have to deal with a serious threat to their physical safety—a frightening encounter with the nation of Amalek.

CHAPTER 20

"Faith" in the Hands of Moses

IT IS HARD TO BELIEVE that anyone would try to attack the Israelites, since just about everyone had heard about the plagues in Egypt and the Israelites' miraculous deliverance from the world's mightiest empire. All the surrounding nations should have known that the Israelites had a powerful protector.

The celebratory Song at the Sea actually enumerated the names of four neighboring nations that were awestruck after hearing how the Israelites had been saved. "The peoples have heard, they tremble; Pangs have taken hold of the inhabitants of Philistia. Then were the chiefs of Edom afraid; The mighty men of Moab, trembling takes hold of them; All the inhabitants of Canaan are melted away."

We would assume that *no* nation would bother them. Yet, we learn that "then came Amalek, and fought with Israel in Rephidim." Why was this nation different from all the others? Why weren't they afraid of confronting the Israelites, who had been saved by God's mighty power? They must have had a different perspective than the other nations, one that motivated them to attack this Divinely protected people.

The Midrash explains that the Amalekites attacked because

they knew something important about their own lineage and the lineage of the Israelites. The people of Amalek recognized that the only reason for the salvation of the Hebrews was the merit of their ancestor, Abraham, with whom God had made a covenant, and for whose sake God was faithful to them. But the Amalekites also knew that unlike the other nations, they were also descended from Abraham. And thus, they were also protected by his merit.

To understand this slightly complicated genealogy, we need to go back to the book of Genesis, where Abraham's family history is elaborated. As you may recall, Abraham's son Isaac became the father of twins—Jacob and Esau. Jacob eventually had twelve sons, including Levi, from whom Moses descended. Meanwhile, Esau fathered Eliphaz, who took a concubine named Timna. This union produced Amalek. So Moses and Amalek were the descendants not only of brothers, but of twins!

The nation of Amalek appreciated this family history. It was also well aware that Jacob had bought the birthright from his brother, Esau, at a time when Esau was hungry and particularly vulnerable, and that some years later, Jacob had received his father's blessing for that birthright by disguising himself as Esau. The Midrash suggests that this was a closely guarded family secret that had been passed down from generation to generation.

After officiating at numerous life-cycle events, I have become acutely aware of how many families share such secrets. After a wedding I conducted some months ago, I was congratulating the nephew of the groom, when his mother walked up with a man at her side. Turning to her son, she said, "I'd like you to meet your first cousin."

Why hadn't they met before? Why have I seen similar scenes reenacted at weddings, bar mitzvahs, and funerals? Somehow, in the course of time, two brothers or sisters, who had grown up on perfectly amiable terms, had stopped speaking to each other. The reasons are always complex, sometimes involving illness or financial matters, or issues of sexual abuse. No matter what the cause, a terrible rift took place, and it was never mended.

That is what I find so tragic about the estrangement between Jacob and Esau. It seems to me that a lot of historic—and contemporary—events relate to this ancient feud. Despite the fact that Jacob and Esau reconciled for a time during their lives and even came together to bury their father, many differences between them were never completely resolved. Total reconciliation was never accomplished. The nation of Amalek—descendants of Esau—still remembered how their birthright had been taken away from them, so they attacked their cousins, the Israelites.

Moses told his assistant Joshua to choose a cadre of men and go out to fight with Amalek. The next day, Moses climbed to the summit of a nearby hill, carrying his rod, the symbol of his empowerment. Accompanying him were his brother Aaron and his nephew Hur. As the Israelites gazed up at Moses, something amazing happened: "When Moses held up his hand, Israel prevailed; and when he let down his hand, Amalek prevailed." The Midrash points out that Moses actually lifted up *both* of his hands, after recognizing that the Israelites needed even more inspiration to overcome their enemies.

Contrary to what we might assume from this simple description, these developments were not the result of any magical abilities that Moses possessed. Rather, his hands served as a symbol of God's Presence and power. The Midrash describes how every time Moses lifted his hands and rod upwards, the Israelites were reminded of the One Who appointed Moses to be leader of His people. They believed that the same God Who led them out of Egypt and performed other miracles for them would empower them to overcome the forces of Amalek.

So even though the people's faith gave them strength, they still needed the inspiration of a great leader. This seems to be the tendency of human beings, even when they believe deeply in a cause for which they are willing to fight.

Moses was the ultimate leader. When the people looked to him, they did not see only the man, but all that he had done and all that he stood for. And most importantly, they knew Who appointed him. But even Moses got tired sometimes. He needed others to help him. Aaron and Hur took a stone and put it under Moses, so that he could sit down. And when his hands became heavy, Aaron stood to one side of him, supporting that hand, while Hur supported the hand on the other side. Moses's hands thereby remained steady and high until the sun went down.

The Bible uses an unusual word—*emunah*—to describe the steadiness of Moses's hands. This word, from the same root as "amen," literally means "faith." Because Moses's hands were faithful—full of faith—they caused the people to believe. And thus, the Israelites defeated Amalek.

THE BIBLE SAVES US FROM DESTRUCTION

Following this military victory, yet another novel event occurred. For the first time, God told Moses to write down something specific to convey to future generations: "Write this for a memorial in the book, and rehearse it in the ears of Joshua: for I will utterly blot out the remembrance of Amalek from under heaven."

This seems to be a pretty harsh dictum, not only for that time but for *all* time. To see it in proper perspective, we need to remember that the covenant with Abraham represents God's *third* attempt at creating a better world. His prior attempts—first with Adam and Eve, then with Noah—did not result in the type of people who could live with each other.

So God continued trying to shape people who would join Him in creating a better world, people who would not oppress each other or tolerate such destructive behavior. He wanted Abraham's descendants to be a light unto the nations, to demonstrate kindness, sensitivity, caring, and compassion. God recognized that a number of other nations—particularly Egypt and Amalek—did not share these values and would try to destroy the Israelites. As an elaboration of this story in Deuteronomy makes clear, Amalek represented the most heartless type of predator, preying on the weak and the weary. That type of external, destructive force was what God was trying to eliminate for all time.

Moses bore witness to this holy plan. He built an altar, where he declared, "The Lord will have war with Amalek from generation to generation."

That prediction conveys an even deeper meaning when we consider that Amalek might represent more than an external enemy. The Israelites' encounter with Amalek can also be understood to suggest that an element of Amalek is present in each one of us. By this, I mean our need for power or other aspects of our "shadow" side, the dark part of ourselves that is not always visible to others—or to ourselves.

After leaving Egypt, the Israelites had struggled initially with physical needs, especially with acquiring water and food. But their next struggle represented a fundamental, nonmaterial concern—dealing with the duality of human nature, the good and the bad. That battle continues today. Whether on an individual or a collective basis, our Divine mandate remains the same. We are to overcome the bad, whether it is within or without.

Essentially, both understandings of Amalek are the same.

No matter how we view the dark aspects of Amalek, we can attempt to overcome and transform them somehow—by redirecting and transcending them. We can be helped in this process by the guidance and laws of the Torah, which exist to teach us how *not* to act from our darkness, how *not* to act like Amalek.

Moses set about the difficult challenge of instructing his followers—about three million people—in how to lead this type of existence. And even though he was a great, inspired leader, the question remained: could he handle this tremendous task all by himself?

CHAPTER 21

Moses—The Teacher of Humanity

AS WE HAVE SEEN with Amalek, family relationships were quite significant in the life of Moses and the history of the Israelites. Fortunately, most of these relationships were positive. For example, Jethro, Moses's father-in-law, made pivotal contributions to Moses's personal life, as well as to his development as the leader of the Israelites.

The Midrash provides an instructive lesson in family relationships by contrasting Amalek with Jethro. Amalek, though related to Moses by blood, completely estranged himself from his cousin and the rest of the Israelites. Not only that, the Amalekites tried to destroy them.

Jethro was a completely different kind of relative. He started out as a stranger, a foreigner, not part of Moses's family at all. The Midrash tells us he enjoyed high social status as an idolatrous priest in Midian. But, after his own ethical, moral, and intellectual explorations, he not only joined Moses and his people, but also became a trusted advisor to Moses.

The differing stories of Amalek and Jethro make clear that the religion of the Hebrews is based not only on biology, but also on ideology, on a shared value system. When outsiders choose to adopt these values and convert, they are welcomed with open arms and appreciated for their new insights. For example, Jethro had much to teach his new people, both through his actions and the way that he interacted with Moses. The two of them enjoyed a long and mutually respectful relationship.

When Jethro first heard about the liberation of the Israelites from the Egyptians, he went out to join Moses and the people in the desert. His thoughts and actions were diametrically opposite those of the people of Amalek: "And Jethro rejoiced for all the goodness which the Lord had done to Israel, in that He had delivered them out of the hand of the Egyptians." Furthermore, Jethro offered a blessing to God. Recognizing all the Divine goodness that had been showered upon the Israelites, Jethro proclaimed: "Blessed be the Lord, who has delivered you out of the hand of the Egyptians, and out of the hand of the pharaoh."

It seems significant that it took an outsider to truly recognize the greatness of what had occurred and to respond to it appropriately. Perhaps that is why an old saying reminds us that, "There is no prophet in your own city." I notice that even today, this tendency remains the same. I see it in myself. I work in a large medical center, furnished with the latest and most sophisticated technological equipment and patient comforts. But after many years at this same institution, I take some of these features for granted. I am used to having things this way.

But several years ago, an outsider helped me appreciate just how much we have at Cedars-Sinai. This superb physician delivered a lecture at our hospital. As I showed him around before his talk, he couldn't get over the facilities and equipment. "Even if our administrators voted in favor of some of this stuff," he said, "it would take ten years to get it all approved." With that reminder, I again appreciated many of the hospital's features. But it took an outsider to give me the right perspective.

BALANCING OUR LIVES

Even though Jethro started out as an outsider, he had been an important part of Moses's life for some time. While Moses struggled against the pharaoh in Egypt, it was Jethro who cared for the family that Moses had left behind in Midian.

As difficult as it may be for us to imagine, Moses had no real family life for a number of years. With the permission of his father-in-law, he put his Divine calling—saving his people—ahead of the needs of his wife and their two sons.

That must have been a terrible conflict for him. Even today, people in leadership positions with fewer and lesser responsibilities than Moses had struggle to juggle their personal and professional lives, trying to maintain some sort of healthy balance. But Moses's situation demanded total, constant, and complete dedication to his mission.

We recognize the tremendous sacrifices that Moses made when we read about his reunion with his family. According to the Midrash, Moses had done more than just leave his wife at her father's home so she would be safe. After the birth of his two sons, Moses had completely abstained from sexual intimacy with her.

Moses is the only person in the entire Bible who took such an extreme step. But he was unique. He was the greatest of the prophets, the only one whom directly encountered God. Furthermore, his mission included being available to God at all times, unlike other prophets. It is clear that it was not possible for him to find a balance between fulfilling God's mission to serve humanity and having a family life.

Moses did not have the opportunity to nurture his children as he would have liked, and they did not have the chance to form a strong bond with him. However, even if Moses's family had remained with him, it does not seem likely that their situation would have been ideal. We have only to look at busy people today to see how their personal lives are disrupted by their work.

Some physicians I know have told me touching stories about the personal costs of being busy professionals. One doctor said that on many Friday evenings, as he and his family usher in the Sabbath, the same thing often occurs. "As I stand there with the cup of wine in my hand, about to pronounce the blessing, my beeper goes off," he lamented. "It never fails, winter or summer, rain or shine. And it hurts me to see what happens to my wife and kids and the whole atmosphere of our home when I disappear into the next room for a lengthy telephone consultation. I know that it's a great privilege to save lives, but look what's happening to my family as a result!"

Such disruptions of normal family life are not limited to physicians, of course. The great South African leader Nelson Mandela once told a journalist how one day, when he tried to hug his grown-up daughter, she flinched away from him and burst out, "You are the father to all our people, but you have never had the time to be a father to me." He said that his greatest regret was the price that his children paid for his political commitments.

As I attempt to understand the circumstances that required Moses's withdrawal from family life, I am saddened by the toll that it must have taken on him, as well as on his family. But, as a friend reminded me, this episode is just another indication of how Moses and the other key figures in the Bible are presented as human beings with real flaws and problems. They are not ascetic figures who go out alone to raise their spiritual consciousness, but people with families, affected by their own life circumstances and those of their dear ones.

Despite Moses's long absence from his family, Jethro remained a devoted and faithful father-in-law. In fact, he was the one who came up with a suggestion that greatly eased Moses's burdens as a leader. Jethro had been not only a Midianite priest, but also an influential leader of that society. He had good administrative skills and knowledge of the judicial process.

Therefore, he became alarmed and mystified when he observed how Moses conducted his "business." Every day, from morning to evening, hundreds of people lined up before the chair where Moses sat to ask for his advice and guidance on a wide range of issues and problems, domestic disputes, and ethical questions. Jethro's moral sensitivity was so great that, according to the Midrash, he admonished Moses for sitting while everyone else stood. He told Moses that by doing this, he was denigrating the honor of the people who came for guidance.

Jethro made a further suggestion. He advised Moses to appoint highly qualified men to help him arbitrate the huge number of cases. The character of these assistant judges had to be beyond reproach. They had to be men who "fear God, men of truth, hating unjust gain." Jethro realized that some cases would still need to be heard by Moses, but he suggested that, "Every *large* matter they will bring unto you, but every small matter they will judge themselves; so will they make it easier for you and bear the burden with you."

Moses heeded the advice of his father-in-law. The description of how this plan was enacted is very instructive, since it varies slightly from Jethro's words. Concerning the lower court judges, we read, "the *difficult* cases they brought unto Moses, but every small matter they judged themselves." The Midrash points out that the change in the words describing Moses's cases—from *"large"* to *"difficult"*—conveys an important lesson about the way a judicial system is supposed to work. Moses and the judges were to disregard litigants' social and economic status and other social characteristics. When a problem was difficult, it was to be brought before Moses—even if it involved the simplest, most humble person in the community.

WE ARE ALL TEACHERS

Jethro recognized Moses's greatness and understood Moses's leadership role. Moses's primary function was to teach, and his role as a teacher was defined in the broadest possible sense. Moses did not just give the people a number of facts to memorize. Rather, Jethro told Moses, "Teach them the statutes and the laws, and you shall show them the way wherein they must walk, and the work that they must do."

The right way to walk through life cannot be defined in dry, legal terms. It encompasses an attitude and a set of behaviors that, when practiced regularly, become almost natural. Moses demonstrated how we should relate to each other in a caring, compassionate manner. We should visit the sick, care for the poor, honor the dead, and teach others what we have been taught. In this way, we make the world a better place.

Similarly, according to the Midrash, "the work that they must do" is not a simple concept at all. What that "work" is to be requires careful study of the human condition. Judges and teachers have to understand the *spirit of the law,* not just the dictates of the law.

As I remind my students, if five people with similar questions appear before the same judge or teacher, they most likely will receive five different answers. These are unique individuals, coming from diverse backgrounds and circumstances, and they *each* possess a unique psyche and understanding of reality. Therefore, all of these variables need to be assessed before an appropriate response can be given.

It was particularly important for Moses to teach the people this crucial concept during this phase of their journey. For as they approached Mount Sinai, where they would receive the Divine teachings, it was essential for them to understand the vital concept of going beyond the letter of the law.

CHAPTER 22

Moses Ascends
and God Descends

I T TOOK THE ISRAELITES seven weeks to walk from Egypt to
Mount Sinai. This was more than just a physical exercise to
get from one place to another. It involved a process of spiritual
elevation from one level to the next, ultimately allowing the
Israelites to reach a state in which they would be ready to experience Divine revelation and receive the Ten Commandments.

The Israelites were not truly liberated when Moses led them
out of slavery. They were timid and afraid of the unknown, constantly thinking back to the security of their lives as slaves. No
matter how many miracles they witnessed—plagues, the splitting
of the sea, manna, and so forth—they still felt very vulnerable.
They did not have adequate faith to sustain them through periods of difficulty. That is why, when they were engaged in battle
with the Amalekites, they had to look to Moses's uplifted hands
to give them the strength they needed to overcome the enemy.

This whole series of events teaches us a great deal about
Moses. No other leader would have had the ability—or desire—
to go on leading this fearful, doubtful people, whose constant refrain was essentially, "Let us return to Egypt." Who would be
willing to put up with these thankless, complaining people?

Anyone else would have been sucked into his followers' cycle of depression, and would ultimately have abandoned them and the mission as well.

But Moses was an extraordinary man. He had experienced the Divine Presence. That episode at the burning bush was inextricably linked to what would later happen at Mount Sinai. As a matter of fact, these two events took place at exactly the same spot—the bush grew at the base of Mount Sinai. At the time of the burning bush, God said, "This will be the sign for you that I have sent you: When you have brought the people out of Egypt, you will serve God upon this mountain."

From that moment on, Moses focused on his singular mission, and he did not let the people bring him down to their level. He had experienced God, and he knew what he had to do. Eventually, his leadership had an effect on the Israelites, and he became the catalyst for their spiritual growth. The people finally repented and changed their behavior.

It is clear that the potential for change, even sudden, dramatic change, always exists. In the right hands, that potential can become actualized. That was the case for Leon, a highly successful business executive, who recently made me aware how an influential leader can bring about the most unexpected results. Leon has made millions of dollars developing and restructuring electronics companies. Several months ago, he was asked to help merge two rival manufacturers in northern California. At first, the proposal seemed hopeless, with both sides locked into their positions and unwilling to compromise.

Then, Leon realized that he "was the only one who knew what was really going on here. We weren't just talking about dollars or reallocations. We had to deal with the insecurities of top management at both firms. So the last time we met, I turned to the officers and vice presidents of both companies and said, 'Let's get to the bottom line. No matter what terms we finally settle on, I will personally guarantee that each of you will maintain your present position and compensation for three years after we finalize the deal.' Within fifteen minutes, I had everybody ready to sign on the dotted line." A complete about-face and change of heart became possible when the process was facilitated by someone with great leadership skills and an understanding of what makes a person tick.

For such events to transpire in the lives of individuals or corporations is quite remarkable. But when an entire people is transformed, it is truly amazing. In the wilderness, *all* the Israelites underwent a deep and significant transformation that prepared them for receiving the Ten Commandments. An allusion to their collective spiritual growth is found in the unusual wording of the text. We read that when the people came to Mount Sinai, "They encamped *[va-yachanu]* in the wilderness; and there Israel encamped *[va-yichan]* before the mount." In the original Hebrew, the first instance of "encamped" is written in the plural form; the second time, the verb appears in the singular. From this variation in language, the Midrash teaches that when the people encamped at the base of Mount Sinai, they were completely united in spirit. They were "as one person, with one heart."

That is quite an incredible statement. I think of my own community today, where small committees can barely meet without dissent and conflicts of opinion. Yet, here in the desert, some two or three million people were thinking and behaving as one. That was truly a spectacular miracle.

It seems that to merit receiving the Bible, the Israelites first had to repent and rectify their behavior. Then, they had to achieve a unified view: "We are one. Our fate is one. We share one heart and one goal." Only then were they ready to receive the commandments at Mount Sinai.

It may seem strange that an out-of-the-way mountain was selected for this holy event. After all, we might have expected this quintessential Divine revelation to happen in Israel, the Promised Land. Yet, choosing this place was actually quite significant. The site for such a unique manifestation must belong to no one. Such a site was open to anybody who wanted to accept the Torah and live according to its teachings. To this day, we really do not know the exact location of Mount Sinai.

MEETING GOD BY TRANSCENDING ALL SEPARATENESS

As the time approached for the Israelites to receive the revelation, "Moses went up *unto God*." Clearly, this verse describes more than just physically climbing up Mount Sinai. From this wording, we understand that Moses had a powerful, transcendent experience at Sinai and was able to bridge the gap between God and humankind.

Most of us experience the loneliness of human existence on a plane that seems very distant from God. To ascend to God, we must be aware of our human limitations, yet strive to unite our human element with the realm of the Divine. But artificial distinctions in language, such as "body" and "soul," cause most of us to continue to think in terms of separateness and divisions in the world.

Furthermore, for many of us it is difficult to see evidence of the Divine in our world. Many generations have been the victims of unspeakable horrors—mass killings and suffering, starvation and deprivation, gang warfare, domestic violence and rape. While we cannot deny these realities, we also need to have a balanced approach to life. Each day, there is much good to behold in the world—the beauty of a flower, a colorful sunset, or a child learning to talk and walk. The same God who hears our cries during our distress is the God who creates beauty and leads us to redemption.

It has been my privilege to encounter a number of people who have achieved this realization in their lives. Many have been patients battling deadly diseases. One woman, Pamela, met with me numerous times throughout her long struggle with leukemia. The disease took a huge toll on her body and spirit. But when she finally entered remission, she became a completely new person. All her activities of daily living—eating, sleeping soundly, speaking with friends, taking walks—became precious again for her.

She would tell me excitedly about the minutiae of her day. "Rabbi, you really should go out and walk today. It's beautiful: not too hot, but you can feel the sun on your back. And the flowers are so colorful. Look at this leaf that I picked off the ground. I wanted you to see it." Pamela reminded me of a child who was seeing things for the first time. She seemed to look at the world as if she had never seen it before, savoring each sight, sound, and moment. This kind of perspective elevates every aspect of life into a meaningful, holy experience.

As Rainer Maria Rilke's title character relates in *The Notebooks of Malte Laurids Brigge:*

> I am learning to see. I don't know why it is, but everything penetrates more deeply into me and does not stop at the place where until now, it always used to finish. I have an inner self of which I was ignorant.

At Mount Sinai, God reminded the people that they had *seen* Divine wonders firsthand—the destruction of the Egyptians and the liberation of God's people. Therefore, their faith was *not* to be based on tradition, tales, written accounts, or other secondary sources. Moreover, God told Moses, "I come unto you in a thick cloud, that the people may *hear* when I speak with you, and may also *believe* you forever." Experience is what matters most; they are to believe because they see, they hear, they know.

It took time for the Israelites to acquire the belief that they had already achieved. Here, at Mount Sinai, God would be revealed in a manner meant to ensure their *continuing* faith, not only in God, but in God's trusted servant, Moses, forever. Accounts of this Divine revelation at Sinai would be transmitted to each succeeding generation. They would include not only what was taught there, but what participants saw, heard, and felt. What better way to ensure the transmission of teachings and beliefs in perpetuity?

Now the people were ready to enter into a wholehearted relationship with God. The terms of this arrangement were straightforward. If they listened to God's voice and kept the covenant, they would be a "kingdom of priests and a holy nation." So, even though members of a particular family had been designated for priestly duties, anyone could fulfill the priestly role of being a servant of God. When everyone achieved this lofty goal, the entire collective would truly become a holy nation.

Until now, not much had been required of the nation as a whole. They primarily had been passive observers rather than active participants. But now, they acted collectively and decisively. When the people were given the choice to enter into this special, privileged relationship with God, they answered immediately, as one: "All that the Lord has spoken we will *do*." The most amazing thing was that they did not even know the particulars of what they were agreeing to! They were accepting the covenantal "package" sight unseen.

Their willingness to proceed was essential to what followed at Mount Sinai—the collective conversion of the Israelites. On that morning, there was loud thunder and lightning, and a thick cloud covered the top of the mountain. A ram's horn—a *shofar*—was sounded, and all the people in the camp trembled. The mountain was surrounded by smoke "because the Lord *descended* upon it in fire."

This is the second time that God chose to appear through the medium of fire. Back at the burning bush, God "descended" also in the guise of fire, which attracted the attention of Moses while he shepherded his flocks. Then, the vision of fire was granted only to Moses. Now, it was a public manifestation, visible to all the Israelites.

The metaphor of fire is very powerful and quite apt. If you get too close to fire, you may be burned, even consumed. If you stay too far away, you will remain cold, isolated, and alienated. The secret is to find just the appropriate balance—the right distance—to feel the warmth, radiance, and light emitted by the flames. That was true at Sinai and it remains true today.

But what happened at Sinai was unique. God became an immanent Presence among the Israelites and, by doing so, disrupted the natural order of the universe. Many of us are familiar with the verse in Psalms, stating, "The heavens are heavens of the Lord; but the earth He has given to the children of men." But at Sinai, this separation between heaven and earth completely disappeared.

The people were now ascending to God. And God was descending, as it were, to them. We see once again that our tendency to separate the components of life is artificial. At this point, the people were united as one, the heavens and earth became one, and the realm of humankind and God was one. All barriers were removed.

This represents the ideal state that had existed back in the Garden of Eden. Even though we experience duality in our lives, our goal is oneness. We think of heaven as separate from earth, but the two realities can be experienced as one. We understand masculine as separate from feminine, but we recognize that when these two forces unite, the result is the birth of a new life, a new beginning. When we find that the duality that we perceive is really part of a united whole, then we will be one within ourselves and with others. And at that time, God's Name will also be one.

CHAPTER 23

Oneness

THE ONENESS OF GOD is a basic premise of the Torah. Yet, at different times, various Names are used to refer to God. These appellations tell us something about God's attributes and characteristics, as well as the way in which we experience and interact with Him throughout our lives. God's Names are significant throughout the Torah, starting from the very beginning in Genesis.

God's revelation to the Israelites at Mount Sinai is not an isolated moment in history. This event is linked to everything that has come before—right back to the beginning of time. The Midrash actually provides a chronology, demonstrating the link between the creation of the world and the happenings at Mount Sinai.

The Bible tells us that the time from Adam to Noah encompassed ten generations. From Noah to Abraham, another ten generations elapsed. From Abraham to Moses, an additional six generations passed by (Abraham, Isaac, Jacob, Levi, Kohath, Amram, and Moses). So, according to tradition, only twenty-six generations separated the first human being from the time of the revelation at Sinai, which took place in the Hebrew year 2448 (1313 B.C.E.).

This link is significant. One of the most striking passages in the Torah relating to God's Name appears at the very beginning of Genesis, in the description of the creation of the world. The wording is brief, yet profound: "In the beginning God created the heaven and the earth." These words are familiar to us, but the English translation does not convey the subtleties of the Hebrew. The Name for God that is used here is *Elohim*—a term associated with judgment, and hence, with reward and punishment.

As seemingly simple as this first verse of the Torah appears, I believe that it teaches us a great and fundamental lesson—God created *both* the heaven and the earth. Similarly, there appears to be duality in other aspects of our lives—body and spirit, masculine and feminine, light and darkness. But the quintessential point of the first verse of the Bible and the creation story is that *what appears as duality emanates from One and is really oneness*.

A similarly significant passage—one that conveys the same lesson—appears at the very beginning of the Ten Commandments. As the people stood at the foot of Mount Sinai, amid the smoke, fire, and quaking of the earth, the Torah tells us, "God [*Elohim*] spoke all these words, saying: I am the Eternal your God, Who brought you out of the land of Egypt, out of the house of bondage."

In the creation story, the Name used to describe God is *Elohim*, the Judge. But at Sinai, God is described in terms of other qualities as well. God used both the Name meaning "Judge" and the one meaning "Eternal." The latter Name conveys compassion and mercy; both reflect various characteristics of the one God.

So at Sinai, it was clear that God was offering a new covenantal relationship—a partnership—with the people liberated from Egypt.

Thus, at the outset, God told the Israelites, in effect: "I am both the Eternal (mercy) and God (judgment). When you crossed the Sea of Reeds, I appeared in the form of a mighty God who wages war. When I appeared at Sinai, I was the master Teacher of Torah. When you experience the different aspects of My Presence, your world may appear to be split. But know that it is all one, just as I am One."

The oneness of God as a central principle of belief is found later on in the book of Deuteronomy, where we read, "Hear, O Israel, the Eternal, our God, the Eternal is one." Why is this most significant statement in the *last* of the Five Books of Moses? After all, almost everything that appears in Deuteronomy restates something that has been in an earlier book. I believe that the "Hear, O Israel" prayer reiterates the central lesson of God's oneness that was taught at Mount Sinai. This is the same "Hear, O Israel" prayer that Jews traditionally recite before death. So the last word uttered by many people—their last conscious thought— is this concept of "one," indicating that even death is part of the larger oneness of life.

GOD EXISTS IN OUR DAILY STRUGGLES

The Midrash clarifies how all of life and the world reflects the Divine oneness. As humans, our perceptions are limited by such concepts as time, space, and separateness. But in the Divine realm, such artificial barriers do not exist. At the same time that God creates birth, eventual death is also created. Similarly, God simultaneously creates sickness and healing, light and dark, good and evil. We tend to look at these as opposite entities, but in reality everything is part of one continuum.

Thus, though every birth is rightly greeted as a joyful event, in it lie the seeds of eventual death. Similarly, light and shadow are related to one another. Sometimes, it is actually hard to differentiate at all between two "opposite" entities. For example, the sun can be in only one position at a given time, so that while some people see light, others observe darkness. Sunrise for one community means sunset for another.

My art teacher was instrumental in helping me see the world in this unified manner. Many years ago, when I first began to study, she complimented me on my drawings. But she also provided constructive criticism about my work. "Levi," she once told me, "your paintings are too full of light. You're leaving out a lot of life. Why don't you try to add some darkness to your pictures? Eventually, you'll discover that shadow is what allows us to see the light."

Over time, I have come to further understand and appreciate my teacher's comments. I can recognize more clearly the oneness that surrounds us. This unity of creation reflects the unity of the Creator, regardless of how many Names we use to identify the Divine. But there is also another message in "I am the Eternal *your God*." Despite the fact that these words were spoken to some two or three million people, the Hebrew word for "your God" appears in the singular, rather than the plural form. The Midrash comments that *each* person is responsible for upholding the values and teachings of the Torah. We cannot say, "Let others fulfill it for me." The Torah may have been given to a collective, but it was also given to each individual.

Some people come to this realization on their own. A few months ago, I visited an elderly patient shortly before his death. For a number of reasons, this man had become quite alienated from any form of Jewish tradition or expression. During our previous visits, he had expressed quite a bit of anger and ridicule about those who maintain these practices. Yet, in what amounted to his deathbed "confession," he told me: "Rabbi, you know I've always said I can't understand a lot of the old ways, or the people who spend their lives studying those things. But I've got to admit that without them, the rest of us wouldn't have made it this far. And it's important that we're here." This man eventually recognized that each of us has an important and significant role to play in carrying out a personal mission that dates back to Sinai. Whether he realized it or not, this patient had absorbed a lesson of the first commandment.

The latter part of this commandment is also instructive. God is identified as the One "Who brought you out of the land of

Egypt, out of the house of bondage." Notice that no mention was made of Moses, who had played such a pivotal role in this process. God made it perfectly clear who is in charge of running the world. It isn't any mortal who serves as God's messenger; God alone directs the events of history. By specifically referring to the Exodus from Egypt, God further clarified that the Divine Presence is involved in the daily lives and struggles of humanity.

The idea of God speaking audibly to a group of people is truly awesome. Even more remarkable is that the biblical description of this event states that the Voice of God that spoke to those people long ago "has never ceased."

Rabbi Dr. Avraham Altmann, the former chief rabbi of Trier, Germany, suggests that the ability to hear God's Voice is directly related to our actions and ethics. Altmann likens that eternal Voice to sound waves being emitted by a radio transmitter. We have to be tuned to the right "frequency" in order to pick them up. Rabbi Altmann, in his "The Meaning and Soul of 'Hear, O Israel,'" explains how we can try to achieve this: "The human without ethics passes by what cries out most in life without hearing, whereas one of high moral character hears even the most subdued call and traces its source."

LEARNING TO LISTEN

Hearing alone is not enough. Acting on the basis of what we hear ultimately determines if we continue to hear the Voice that emanated from Sinai. But how can we listen effectively to begin with? In working with my clients, I have become increasingly aware that much of what we hear is filtered through—and distorted by—"background noises," such as the voices of our parents or other significant people in our lives. Yet, by practicing meditative or other techniques to center ourselves before praying, we can become better attuned to voices of inspiration. Competing voices and influences become less distracting as we allow ourselves to be completely receptive to interaction with God. In that way, we can strive to envision ourselves at Sinai.

Some people are confused by those first words uttered at Mount Sinai. After all, they introduce a body of commandments that serve as guidelines for living. But the first sentence identifying God seems to be not so much a guideline as a statement of fact. Is it one of the Ten Commandments or merely an introduction to what follows?

A number of commentators have concluded that God's way of self-identifying is, in fact, a commandment. I agree with this view, and I translate those initial words at Sinai as follows: "I, the Eternal, am to be your God." This is not a simple statement of belief. This is the description of a continuing process that requires a great deal of work on our part. The more we live an ethical life, the more we will come to recognize God as our personal God. And the motivating factor for us to lead that kind of life will be our continued hearing of that Divine Voice from Sinai.

At Sinai, there was oneness of Divinity and humanity. This ideal state is something that we can aspire to and strive to realize throughout our lives. We cannot control where and when God may descend to us, but we can try to ascend as high as we can.

While Moses ascended Mount Sinai, the rest of the people were camped at the foot of the mountain. Their leader, Moses, who had been with them throughout every test and ordeal that they had endured, was now out of sight. The Israelites had already heard "You shall have no other gods besides Me. You shall not make for yourself a graven image." They had already proclaimed that they would follow all the commandments. But in the temporary absence of Moses, these people—who had witnessed and heard the most amazing things—began to forget all that they had seen and heard. And they began to fear that they had been abandoned.

PART IV

Kindness and Compassion

CHAPTER 24

Betrayal

WHEN MOSES ASCENDED Mount Sinai, he let the Israelites know he would be away for forty days and forty nights. They carefully kept track of the days that Moses was away, and on the fortieth day, they eagerly looked forward to his return. But they neglected to take into account the fortieth night that he had mentioned. And so, toward the end of the fortieth day, they became more and more concerned. They began to worry that Moses would never return. In their morbid fantasies, they began to fear the worst. They noticed that no manna fell on Mount Sinai and wondered if perhaps Moses had starved or died some other horrible death. They worried that they would never see him again, this leader on whom they were so totally dependent.

Their all-too-human response should strike a chord of recognition in all of us. Imagine being a parent of a teenager who has just obtained a driver's license. It's Saturday night, and the teenager promises to drive extra cautiously and return home no later than midnight. By 11:00 p.m., you are anxious and getting more so with each tick of the clock. You start listening to the radio for any bulletins about traffic accidents. By the time your child arrives home, you may have called all the local emergency rooms, the police department, and the highway patrol. Every additional moment had exponentially increased the worst of your fears.

This is the state of mind that overtook the Israelites waiting at the base of Mount Sinai. They thought "that Moses delayed to come down from the mount," and a panic attack set in.

As the Midrash describes in extensive detail, they had just participated in a "wedding" ceremony with God, Who had liberated them and made them into a people. God was the groom; the people were the bride; the Torah would be the marriage contract; the two tablets of the Law, containing the Ten Commandments, would represent the two witnesses essential to the ceremony; Mount Sinai was the marriage canopy; and the bride's jewelry was the entire body of law and teachings that was being transmitted to the people.

This should have been a blissful occasion, complete with mutual trust and love. But when Moses appeared to be late in returning from the top of the mountain, what followed was disastrous.

The people gathered around Aaron, telling him: "Make us a god who will go before us; for as for this Moses, the man that brought us up out of the land of Egypt, we know not what is become of him." They wanted a tangible "god" that would be with them at all times.

What the people told Aaron indicated that they still did not "get it." They had already heard the Divine Voice proclaim "I am the Eternal, your God, Who brought you out of the land of Egypt," yet they had quickly forgotten this essential belief.

RECOGNIZING OUR LIMITS

One of the most difficult lessons of life is that we cannot have whatever we want whenever we want it. In the Garden of Eden, Adam and Eve could have just about anything, except for the fruit from one forbidden tree. And, of course, *that* was exactly what they craved. Now that the people had entered into a holy cove-

nant with God, they had been promised some very wonderful re-
wards. In return, the one basic belief that they had to uphold
was to recognize God and not have any other gods besides this
God. And *that* is what they now found difficult to do. All of us
tend to yearn for what is forbidden, and the Israelites were no
exception.

The Israelites acted on their desires. While Aaron tried to stall
them, the people proceeded with their plans to create a graven
image. They collected gold jewelry, melted it down, and it was
mysteriously fashioned into a golden calf. Then the people proclaimed before the calf, "These are your gods, O Israel, which
brought you up out of the land of Egypt." Their actions make me
think of the classic definition of *chutzpah*, which is generally
translated as "gall." Someone once described it as a man mur-
dering both his parents, then throwing himself on the mercy of
the court because he is an orphan! What the Israelites did was
worse than *chutzpah*. It was total betrayal.

The "bride"—Israel—was being unfaithful to her "husband"—
God—on their wedding night. In addition to turning to idolatry,
the Israelites publicly proclaimed the very *opposite* of the Divine
teaching that Moses would bring down from Sinai—that *God*
brought them out of Egypt. The people also engaged in other
forbidden activities. They begin to mimic the pagan rituals they
had seen in Egypt, and their idol worship was soon accompanied
by licentious behavior and even murder.

Idolatry was not unique to the Israelites, nor was it limited to
ancient times. While the actions of many people today may not
be quite so extreme, at times they resemble some type of idolatrous worship. Perhaps because I live in southern California, I am
particularly aware of how the pursuit of happiness—and in particular, eternal youth—has become almost a religious quest. I encounter many people who have undergone extensive plastic and
reconstructive surgeries, thinking that these procedures will mag-
ically transform their bodies and their lives. Perfect love will be

achieved, professional achievement attained, and social acceptance guaranteed if only tucks are taken here, fat suctioned there,
and a little bit of collagen injected into just the right spots. Isn't
this search for bodily perfection sometimes a form of self-
worship? There are many types of golden calves around today,
even though we do not always recognize them as such.

IDOLATRY BETRAYS GOD

At Sinai, however, the people's idolatry was unambiguous.
Likewise, God's reaction to it was swift and severe. He ordered
Moses to go back down the mountain. The Midrash explains that
Moses was actually being excommunicated from the Divine
Presence. He was being treated as an outcast. God spoke to him
in very harsh terms: "Go, get you down; for *your* people, that *you*
brought up out of the land of Egypt, have dealt corruptly." Notice
the unusual choice of pronouns in this verse. In the first of the
Ten Commandments, God is self-identified as the One who liberated the people from Egypt. Yet here, they became *Moses's* people. God was backing away from them, starting "divorce" pro-
ceedings against them.

One of my students suggested that all of these problems could
have been avoided if, when Moses did not return, the anxious
Israelites had simply selected Aaron to take Moses's place. As
Moses's brother, he would have been a natural choice. However,
not everyone possessing great qualities is fit to lead. The Midrash
describes Aaron as a wonderful person—full of compassion and
kindness, and quick to make peace with others and teach others
to do likewise. But someone so kind, with the desire and ability
to get along with everyone, is probably not suited to be a leader.
After all, a leader has to make unpopular decisions, sometimes
alienating others in the process. Furthermore, a leader requires
special strength, sometimes needing to act in very unkind ways.
Early in his life, when he killed an Egyptian oppressor, Moses had

demonstrated that he had the strength, as well as the compassion, to lead his people to freedom and beyond.

Moses now had the opportunity to use his leadership ability in yet another critical situation. He entered into a unique dialogue with God, Who was furious. God tells Moses: "Now therefore *allow Me,* that My wrath may wax hot against them, and that I may consume them; and I will make of you a great nation."

At this juncture, the all-powerful God asked Moses for permission to act! Since when does God need Moses's approval? God appeared to be asking Moses to help ensure that Divine wrath would not dominate Divine actions. This was quite extraordinary. God was empowering people, as it were, to influence God's decisions!

God still desired to make the world a better place, and to that end, was even willing to destroy the very people whom God had chosen. God made Moses an extraordinary offer. God proposed to get rid of the Israelites and start all over again, making Moses the head of a new great nation. Moses proved his greatness by not even pausing to consider this possibility. He thought of the well-being of the entire nation, rather than about his own ego. Furthermore, Moses demonstrated that he had grown dramatically as a leader since he had first been selected for his mission. As we saw earlier, Moses had at first been reluctant to accept his calling and required repeated reassurances from God before he took on the great task of leading the people. Now, in an ironic role reversal, Moses tried to "convince" God to proceed with the original mission for which the Israelites had been chosen.

Moses prayed to God, and his prayer was ingenious. In it, he invoked God's very own statements in order to argue his case. He began by "reminding" God that these were still God's people who had been liberated: "Why does Your wrath wax hot against *Your* people, that *You* have brought forth out of the land of Egypt with great power and with a mighty hand?" Furthermore, Moses remembered that throughout the plagues and Exodus from Egypt, God had repeated again and again why Divine existence and powers were being made known to the Egyptians and the surrounding nations. Now, Moses suggested that the Egyptians would say that the Israelites had been brought out of slavery only so God could "slay them in the mountains, and consume them from the face of the earth." Moses pleads, "Turn from Your fierce wrath, and renounce the plan to punish Your people."

Moses continued to bring up the issues that had been God's recurring themes throughout the generations: "Remember Abraham, Isaac, and Israel, Your servants, to whom You did swear by Your own self, and said unto them: 'I will multiply your seed as the stars of heaven, and all this land that I have spoken of will I give unto your seed, and they shall inherit it for ever.'"

Moses's arguments were successful. "And the Lord renounced the punishment which He said He would do unto His people." But the crisis was not yet over. First, Moses had to descend from Sinai and confront those who had turned to idolatry and immorality in the midst of this holy encampment.

Moses went down the mountain, carrying the two tablets of the Law—the work of God—in his hands. As soon as he came into the camp, he saw the people dancing and worshiping the golden calf. He became very angry and threw down the tablets, smashing them at the base of the mountain. Then he called upon all those who remained loyal to God to join him. All the sons of Levi gathered together with Moses and, following God's law and Moses's orders, killed three thousand men who had participated in the hedonistic, idolatrous rituals. This time of Divine revelation and "marriage"—which should have been a peak spiritual experience—became, instead, marred with violence and bloodshed.

The following day, Moses climbed the mountain again, this time to seek complete atonement for what the people had done. He wanted to rebuild a relationship of trust between God and the people, but he was only partially successful.

Moses acknowledged to God that the people had indeed sinned grievously. But then he issued God an ultimatum, saying that if the Israelites were not forgiven, then God should erase Moses's name from the biblical narrative. Moses seemed to be saying that if forgiveness was not forthcoming, he did not want anything further to do with God.

God responded succinctly, telling Moses, "Whosoever has sinned against Me, him will I blot out of My book." He made it clear that even Moses could not talk to Him this way. God, Who had already promised not to destroy the people, now promised to remain with them, but in a different way. God's angel, who represented a slightly lower level of Divine Presence, would accompany the nation, but God would no longer be as intimately connected with them as in the past.

TRUST IS FRAGILE AND BETRAYAL IS HUMAN

The people's infidelity had tremendous repercussions, not just at the time it occurred, but forever. God made it clear that the betrayal at Sinai would never be forgotten. Divine anger at any future Israelite transgressions would be heightened by God's remembering how the people had behaved at the time of the "wedding" at Sinai.

This seemingly harsh reaction reflects the reality of relationships. In my work as a psychologist, I am particularly aware of certain patterns of behavior. Betrayal is part of the universal fabric of life. The sad truth is that in every relationship involving love and trust, there exist the seeds of betrayal. Everyone in a loving relationship will eventually betray the other, either physically—such as the Israelites' worship of the golden calf—or psychically, with fantasies that exist but are not acted out.

With proper communication, understanding, and a commitment to act differently, such betrayals can be repaired. However, the new bond of trust is different from what existed before. It will never be as complete as it was. It is built upon the reality of experience rather than on innocent hopes and dreams.

I witnessed just such cycles in the lives of a couple who recently came to me for marital counseling. Al and Sue had dated since they were in college. No one was surprised when, ten years ago, they announced their engagement and began to make wedding plans. They set a date for a Sunday in July, planning an entire weekend of activities for their out-of-town guests before the ceremony. Some of the groom's friends took him out for a last fling on Saturday night. Al had too much to drink, and after visiting a strip club, he had sexual relations with a prostitute. Sue wasn't sure exactly what had happened, but after hearing some crude remarks from his friends, she began to wonder just what the "boys" had been up to. But she was not going to let those "unfounded suspicions" get in the way of her big day.

The wedding went ahead as scheduled. Al and Sue moved into their dream home and began to build their family. They had three children—two boys and a girl. But those old issues of betrayal have never gone away.

Such are the complexities of life and of love. Bewilderment and confusion are part of human relationships, just as they are in relationships between humanity and Divinity. As we have seen, Moses was not sure how to proceed in the aftermath of the Israelites' betrayal of God, but he continued to look for answers to guide him along his journey. Eventually, he decided to ask God the ultimate question: What is life all about?

CHAPTER 25

The Ultimate Question

Throughout his life, Moses maintained a singular relationship with God. He repeatedly experienced Divine revelation in a direct way that differed from other prophets' dreamlike visions. However, Moses was still human, still limited in what he could learn about God and the mysteries of life.

It appears that even after God had granted the people atonement, things were not as they had been before. The hurt caused by the nation's straying from God lingered. God and the nation may have been back together again, but their relationship was now different.

An angel would be sent, but God would not accompany the Israelites as they went up to the Promised Land. God was concerned that anger would be overwhelming: "I will send an angel before you . . . if I go up into the midst of you for one moment, I shall consume you."

When the Israelites heard that God would not be among them, they began to mourn. They removed all their ornaments to demonstrate their grief. While witnessing the collective mourning all around him, Moses pondered his own excommunication from the Divine, realizing that he had to work on ascending back to God's realm. This would not happen overnight, and it would require greater efforts on his part. Moses further recognized that while he was distanced from God, he could no longer serve and teach the people in the same way that he had before.

Therefore, Moses removed his tent from its customary place and pitched it outside the camp. He did not actively teach his followers, but those who wanted to learn could seek him out. He continued this arrangement until he and God became reconciled.

Moses's actions and reactions echo patterns of human relations that we continue to see today. I think of my good friend, Valerie, who has volunteered for an important medical charity for the past twenty years. This organization has always valued her hard work and dedication to its cause. But three years ago, a crisis of sorts developed in planning the annual dinner. Valerie and her colleagues, many of whom she had brought into the organization, had some serious disputes about where and when to hold the event, who was qualified to be the honoree, and even the financial goal for this major fundraising gala. Valerie had organized this event for so many years that she trusted her own instincts, but she could not adequately explain these gut-level choices to her associates.

When Valerie was overruled, she decided that she would see this project through to completion for the sake of the cause. But she was deeply hurt. She found it hard to believe that those around her, who had always respected her judgment, now demonstrated doubt and a lack of loyalty. After the dinner that year, she quit the organization, explaining that her heart was just not in her work anymore. Fortunately, with the passage of time and the realization that this charity meant so much to her, Valerie was eventually persuaded to rejoin the group and reassume her leadership position.

Such is the nature of reconciliation. Even though it can often be achieved, it takes time, effort, and great understanding by everyone involved.

When Moses took steps to repair his relationship with God, God heeded his actions. God also noticed that the people continued to demonstrate their love and respect for Moses as their leader. Each time Moses walked to his tent, "all the people rose up, and stood, every man at his tent door, and looked after Moses, until he was gone into the tent."

God also took steps to further the process of reconciliation. Now, when Moses entered his tent, the pillar of cloud—representing the Divine Presence—arrived at the tent door. God then spoke to Moses. The form of their Divine-human interaction was unique: "And the Lord spoke unto Moses face to face, as a man speaks unto his friend."

The results of this intimate dialogue were remarkable. Moses reminded God that at the burning bush, God was introduced by the Name "Eternal," which represented Divine compassion. Moses relied on that quality as he reminded God that the people needed Divine guidance and that they were God's nation.

God responded positively to Moses, promising that all of the Divine Presence—literally, God's "face"—would accompany the people again. That was a wonderful, comforting promise. But Moses sought something even greater. "Show me," he begged, "I pray You, Your glory." Moses wanted to understand the essence of God and all of God's ways.

That is the central, recurring question that I hear over and over again every day, particularly at the hospital where I work. This query encompasses other fundamental questions that we continually ask ourselves as we go through life: Why do things happen the way they do? How can evil befall good people, and good come to evildoers? How can we see the reflection of a compassionate God in this world?

God's response is comforting, yet mysterious: "I will be gracious to whom I will be gracious, and will show mercy on whom I will show mercy. . . . You cannot see My face, for man shall not see Me and live." But God told Moses to station himself in the cleft of a nearby rock. From there, after God's glory had passed by, Moses saw God's back, but the Divine face would remain unseen.

A rabbi I know once used a simple analogy to help explain the unseen face of God. One of his congregants had asked why we can never really see or know God. The rabbi took the man outside and asked him to look at the sun. "I can't do that," the man replied. "It's too bright. It will blind my eyes."

"You're right, of course," said the rabbi. "But you must realize something. If you can't look at the sun—merely one of God's creations—how much more impossible is it for you to look directly at God."

THE BENEFIT OF HINDSIGHT

God's enigmatic reply to Moses about looking at Him describes the unfathomable, unknowable aspect of the Divine. God is compassionate, but we can never know when or why or to whom God will show mercy and compassion. There is no formula, no way to predict it. There is such a gap between finite humanity and the infinite God that it is impossible for us to see these mysterious manifestations of "God's face."

Furthermore, we can only understand God from looking at God's "back." What can this mean? After all, God, Who is incorporeal, is described in anthropomorphic terms only so we can attempt to understand God. But perhaps this allusion to God's "back" suggests that we can only grasp some things in hindsight. Lacking prophetic vision, we can only respond to events. Sometimes, by looking backwards, we can make out a pattern that seems to explain why things happened the way they did.

Several examples come to mind. A patient, Ellen, recently came to see me after she was diagnosed with an early stage of breast cancer. "I can't believe this happened to me," she cried out. "There's not one risk factor or any history in my entire family. This is just crazy. I feel as if the doctors are talking about somebody else." Despite Ellen's initial shock and anger, she was relieved to learn that her treatment would involve only a lumpectomy and some radiation therapy. Now that she has completed these procedures, it is interesting to see how her perspective has shifted dramatically.

"I can't begin to tell you how fortunate I feel," she told me. "My surgery was minimal, and the treatment wasn't bad at all. Every day when I went to the cancer center, I realized how much easier I had it than most of the people around me. But more than that, I'm aware of how lucky I was to catch this thing before it spread. Once it becomes invasive, things can get a whole lot worse. I never used to examine myself regularly, and now, I'm being checked constantly by my doctor and my surgeon. I hope that we'll successfully stop anything else before it can become dangerous. This early warning may be the best thing that ever happened to me."

Ellen's perspective is certainly healthy and life-affirming. Often, hindsight can clarify that a seemingly "bad" event was indeed a blessing in disguise, though such a process may still be very challenging.

Dan told me about a recent trip that he made on the San Diego freeway. He was on his way to an important reception, and it was one of those days when everything seemed to be going wrong. He left the office later than expected, so traffic was heavier than usual. At one point, a large truck skidded and flipped over, blocking several lanes of traffic. Finally, about an hour from downtown Los Angeles, Dan got a flat front tire. Cursing and sweating, Dan pulled over to the shoulder of the road, whipped out his cellular phone, and called the auto club. Forty minutes later, they finally got to him and changed his tire.

When an exhausted Dan finally reached the freeway off-ramp that he planned to take, he found that the way was blocked by barriers, flares, police and fire vehicles, and news vans. A television helicopter circled overhead. A major accident had occurred there. As Dan took an alternate route, he listened to the radio traffic report and learned what had happened. Just around the time that he would normally have reached that freeway exit, a serious collision had taken place there between an oil tanker and several cars. Several people had been taken to nearby hospitals, one with burns over 70 percent of his body. When Dan finally arrived at the reception, his colleagues were greatly relieved to see him. He began to feel that his delay might not have been such a "bad" thing after all, but he only realized that in the aftermath of his experience.

I'm sure that you have experienced something similar in your life. Each of us has to search for our own understanding of this concept of the "back of God." My friend Aviva explained her perspective this way: "This understanding frees me in my daily life from being so afraid. At the moment I'm facing something, I don't know what its true nature really is. Only with some time will I be able to evaluate what happened and see where it led me."

Aviva's understanding gives her the strength and courage to face the challenges and uncertainties of each day. But for all of us, the essential questions of "why" remain unanswerable and unfathomable. Some philosophers point out that this puzzle is actually a blessing. The only way that life can be lived is because of this mystery, this challenge. It becomes the *raison d'être* for most of us. As we endure daily uncertainty, we can only hope and pray that our perspective will enable us to see the most painful events in our lives with greater clarity.

It is the sad nature of existence that we do not always experience the world as a happy, joyful place. At times, we see what appears to be God's "dark side," and we want to run away. But even then, we can find some comfort in the knowledge of another aspect of God's nature: "I will be gracious to whom I will be gracious, and will show mercy on whom I will show mercy." Furthermore, even though we cannot see God's face, we can still engage in dialogue with God, trying to see behind the thin curtain that separates us. Even though we cannot look directly at the ultimate source of illumination, we can at least try to glimpse the light.

CHAPTER 26

Complete Forgiveness

ALTHOUGH THE WAYS OF GOD will always remain mysterious and unfathomable, God enables us to interact with the Divine throughout our lifetimes. The Torah shows us how to coexist with God and with our fellow mortals in every place and in every age. For example, it teaches us to see betrayal as a natural part of the human condition. It is something that will always be with us. And it teaches us how to act after betrayal takes place. Some might look at the initial giving of the Ten Commandments as a colossal failure. After all, this pinnacle event of revelation, which had been planned even before the creation of the world, according to the Midrash, was also a time of idolatry and immorality.

However, there is another way to look at this whole episode. If we interpret it differently, we may find that it is actually quite instructive in letting us know which strategies succeed—and which do not—in healing damaged relationships. For after God's wrath had abated, God decided to offer another revelation, but in a new and different manner, since the first attempt had not been successful.

God decided to transmit the Ten Commandments and the

rest of the Torah once again, but with a number of significant changes. One difference was immediately expressed quite clearly. This time, God told Moses, "Hew for yourself two tablets of stone like unto the first." So, right away, there was a major distinction between the first set of commandments and the second. The first tablets of the Law were the handiwork of God. They were entirely Divine. But the second tablets were hewn also by Moses.

God persisted in his relationship with the people in an attempt to create a better world, but it took on a new form. The language used in the expression "hew for yourself" illustrates part of that change. The Hebrew verb for "hew" *(pesol)* is from the same root as the word for "graven image" *(pesel)* that is used in the second commandment: "You shall have no other gods besides Me. You shall not make for yourself a graven image."

This terminology recognized that the people had gone astray by worshiping an image of a calf. God's new instructions to Moses took into account the human need to have something to touch to relate to the transcendent God. The message seemed to be: "May you never again need to resort to a molten calf or some other idolatrous image to worship. But if you do need something finite, here are these tablets which you have helped hew."

God's wisdom in allowing for a concrete reality is something that I have respect for each day in my practice. In my office, many clients seem to find the theoretical solutions they are seeking. They appear to be very clear about which aspects of their behavior are constructive and which are self-defeating and harmful. Then they return to the outside world, where they re-encounter the concrete realities of their lives—spouses, parents, children, partners, friends. Inevitably, my clients behave in ways that are different from those they imagined back in my office. They realize that what they learn in therapy must also be concretized step-by-step with the flesh-and-blood people who touch their bodies and souls.

MERCY TAKES US TO A HIGHER REALM

Another truth that was revealed in the giving of the second set of commandments pertains to the public and the private realms that each of us experiences. When Moses ascended Mount Sinai to receive the first set of tablets, he was accompanied by others for part of the way—Aaron and his sons, Joshua and seventy elders. They represented the Israelite nation. But the second tablets of the law were given in a completely private setting. Moses was instructed, "no man shall come up with you, neither let any man be seen throughout all the mount."

Private moments are very different from public ones. The Midrash points out that when we share something wonderful with others, a strange phenomenon takes place. Outwardly, people may congratulate us and slap us on the back. But inwardly, others are often envious. This type of jealousy, caused by sharing something special with others, is what the Midrash calls the "evil eye."

This concept is not limited to any one culture or period in history. For example, in a recent interview with the *Los Angeles Times*, Japanese film director Masayuki Suo used similar language to explain how this phenomenon applies in his country:

> Japan is the kind of country where if you walk down the street with a smile on your face, people think that you're boasting. In my own case, I've had lots of wonderful things happen to me on account of this film, and I want to be really happy and rejoice—but it's better that I look like something sad has happened to me, and I walk around looking miserable, otherwise people will complain!

My late Jungian analyst, Dr. James Kirsch, used his own terminology to discuss how he felt about sharing wonderful news, or even a particularly meaningful dream. He always advised adhering to a policy of "containment"—holding back some of your own excitement when you feel that things are going particularly well. By doing so, you will prevent others from being jealous of you.

No matter what our reasons may be for keeping things to ourselves, we usually come to recognize that it is the private moments that are ultimately special in our lives. And in private moments—such as those granted to Moses while in the Divine Presence—the "evil eye" cannot operate.

God took an additional reality into account before giving the Ten Commandments a second time. God recognized that the creation of a better world needed the participation of humanity, despite the ever-present human frailties. God understood that humans will often stumble as they try to ascend to a higher realm. So God now presented Himself in a completely new way.

When Moses ascended to the top of Sinai, God's Presence descended and passed before him, proclaiming twice the compassionate Name, *"Adonai, Adonai,"* "the Eternal One, the Eternal One." The Midrash explains the repetition of this Name by noting that God is the Lord of compassion before we go astray and remains the Lord of compassion even after we have sinned.

The most remarkable feature of this double use of the compassionate Name is that it differs from God's very own first commandment. Earlier, God was presented to the people as both *Adonai,* eternally compassionate, and *Elohim,* the great Judge.

However, the second giving of the Law took place on Yom Kippur, a day of complete compassion and forgiveness. God seemed to have concluded that there could be no Divine relationship with humanity if judgment was involved. From now on, dealings between God and humanity would be based entirely on God's qualities of compassion, mercy, slowness to anger, and abundant loving-kindness.

If that is the way that God has chosen to be revealed to us, it is certainly appropriate behavior for us to emulate. So the only way that we can properly relate to others is through compassion. If we are judgmental, as we so often tend to be, we completely miss the boat and will only create dissension in the world.

One nineteenth-century rabbi suggested how we can behave

compassionately. He pointed out that most of us spend our time looking after our own material comforts, while worrying about the spiritual needs of others. He said that the ideal situation is just the reverse. We should spend our time worrying about the physical needs of others, while looking after our own spiritual needs.

WE ALL REFLECT THE CREATOR

Moses enjoyed the closest possible relationship with God. When he descended from Mount Sinai after receiving the second set of commandments, his face glowed with the light of the Divine Presence. When Aaron and the rest of the Israelites saw this, they were awestruck and afraid. So Moses covered his face with a veil when he spoke to the people and removed it when he conversed with God. The Midrash tells us he continued to do this for the rest of his life.

How are we to understand this manifestation of Divine light? I believe that it is an apt description of the way we transfer energies to and from each other. When we talk at length to someone who is anxious or depressed, we emerge with some of those same feelings. They are just as contagious as diseases conveyed by physical organisms. Conversely, however, we can try to achieve that same special radiance on our faces that Moses achieved. For after all, we are a reflection of our Creator. Rabbi Shlomo Carlebach, the late Hasidic master, described how a sad face reflects God's "sadness." But when we glow with happiness, we remind others of God's "joy." As human beings, we each carry the Divine Image within ourselves.

As we have seen, our experience of the Divine Presence continues to change and manifest itself differently throughout our lives. That is one of the reasons that the second commandment prohibits making any idols or other images of the Divine. Such depictions are fixed, unchangeable, and unmoving. But God's message is quite the opposite. We will continue to experience God in many ways, although the Divine essence will always remain compassionate and caring.

During the giving of the first tablets, the Torah was presented as law, judgment, prescriptions, and protocols. During the second revelation, the Law was presented in a different way—as an ideal. This time, God recognized that humans will continue to struggle, that they are vulnerable and frail, that they will fall from time to time. Yet God needs them to help create a better world, to pick up, as Rabbi Jeffrey Salkin wrote in *Being God's Partner: How to Find the Hidden Link Between Spirituality and Your Work*, "Where God left off . . . this very powerful God needs us to be a partner in the unfolding, incomplete piece of creation. We are not, therefore, insignificant specks in the cosmos. We are nobility."

In addition to helping hew the second tablets, Moses was also commanded: "Write *you* these words." However, God had also told Moses, "*I* will write upon the tablets the words that were on the first tablets."

The Midrash resolves this seeming contradiction in two ways. First, it may be that God wrote the Ten Commandments, while Moses transcribed the rest of the Torah as dictated by God. However, there is a second explanation that I like even better: God and Moses wrote down the words together. With that understanding, our role as human beings becomes clearer. Unique among all of creation, we contain sparks of the Divine Presence. Our goal is to work as partners with God in an attempt to make the world a better place. And when we do, our faces beam with Divine light.

CONCLUSION

Ten Central Lessons

Ten Central Lessons

THE GREAT REVELATION that Moses experienced on Mount Sinai occurred when he was eighty years old. We picture him now as he was then, his face shining with the reflected light of Divine radiance. He had completed the most important part of his mission—leading the Israelites out of Egypt to help them receive the Divine teachings that would guide them and all people throughout the generations. Moses had, indeed, become the teacher of humanity.

Now we can assess the life of this greatest of all prophets. His legacy endures not only in the teachings that he transmitted to his followers. His very life is instructive. It teaches us about ourselves—about our role in life, our struggles, and our relationship with our Creator. Moses's journey enables us to understand more clearly some basic aspects of our existence. Just as he dared to ask the unanswerable, we also spend our days asking: what is life all about?

We, too, seek to understand our role in creating ourselves, as well as our place in God's great design. Many people think of creation as a distant, one-time event that is long over and done with. However, all of life is actually a continuing process of re-creation and rebirth. And it is not a journey that we undertake alone.

During the birthing process, a woman is often assisted by someone who can offer skilled help and guidance—a midwife. Similarly, during the daily re-creation of life and the world, God relies, as it were, on our help. We are God's midwives, God's partners. We each have the potential to be partners with God, to use our unique gifts and skills to help make the world a better place. Whether we are locksmiths, silversmiths, interior decorators, or biomedical researchers; whether we are single, married, divorced, or widowed; whether we are a father or a mother, a sister or a brother, we each have a special contribution to make to this holy process.

A famous tale about a saintly rabbi, Reb Zushia, illustrates the importance of each one of us. It also describes the challenge we each face in trying to live up to our unique God-given potential. As the scholarly and pious Reb Zushia lay on his deathbed, he was crying and inconsolable, despite the comforting words of his students. Finally, he admitted that he was afraid.

"Reb Zushia," the students responded, "your life has been exemplary, filled with learning and doing acts of loving-kindness on behalf of others. Why would you be afraid?"

Reb Zushia replied, "I am not afraid that I will be asked, 'Why were you not as great as Moses?' I am also not afraid that I will be asked, 'Why were you not as great as Aaron or Solomon?' I am afraid I will be asked, 'Why were you not the Reb Zushia you could have been?'"

Reb Zushia's words ring true. How difficult it is to actually live up to the potential with which each of us has been endowed. However, whether we are a Reb Zushia or an Abraham, or an absolutely ordinary person, we can each strive to be an active partner with God in re-creating the world daily. The role model par excellence for this type of partnership is Moses.

On some level, most of us have been exposed to the instructions, guidance, and laws contained in the Ten Commandments that Moses brought down from Mount Sinai. When I review the story of Moses's life, however, I am also struck by ten central lessons that he himself conveys about how to live a meaningful life.

Don't perceive yourself as a victim.

We live at a time and in a society where much can—and is—blamed on our circumstances. It is easy to attribute every failure and difficulty in life to deprivation, mistreatment, or oppression. How many courtroom defenses are based on what Harvard law professor Alan Dershowitz terms "the abuse excuse"? But as people learn in Psychology 101, "when you're in pain, you blame."

Moses could have focused on being born at the time of a genocidal decree; on being sent to an uncertain fate while floating in a basket on a river; on being nursed only intermittently; on growing up in two cultures; as well as on numerous other deprivations and hardships. Yet, he didn't dwell on these hardships. Rather, from early adulthood, he got involved in alleviating the suffering of others, using his own understanding of pain to increase his empathy for the abused. Moses reminds us that we each have the freedom—within some inborn limitations—to choose our way in life. The Torah suggests that we select life-affirming options. We are explicitly told, "choose life, that you may live, you and your seed."

Develop your psyche or Higher Self.

The experience of Divine revelation at the burning bush stayed with Moses all his life, inspiring and directing him when he did not know how to deal with new challenges.

It was Moses's willingness to turn toward the burning bush that led him to an encounter with God. As the Midrash points out, many others walked past that same spot, without noticing anything unusual. But Moses saw the bush, drew nearer to it, and expressed his willingness—"*Hineni,* Here I am." He was ready to do whatever was asked of him.

Perhaps Moses was prepared for the development of his psyche—his inner reality—by his many years of work as a shepherd before his experience at the bush. Out in the desert, in solitude, he had the opportunity to explore his inner life and become comfortable with himself.

The twentieth century does not usually allow opportunities for this type of solitary growth. However, we can make time for personal reflection, meditation, or prayer in order to know ourselves better and to learn to live with ourselves. Periods of self-imposed silence are also helpful in achieving this more highly attuned state. Friends of mine who have gone on silent retreats report tremendous inner growth and peace as a result of their experiences.

I suggest that all of us try to go for long walks, listen to music, or do whatever else most helps us to focus on our inner self and allows us to get in touch with our own psyche.

Face your challenges.

Throughout Moses's life, he faced one challenge after another. He was born into a society that wanted to kill him, so his mother had to hide him for the first months of his life. Then, he was set adrift on the Nile, from which he was plucked by the pharaoh's daughter, who adopted him. He was raised in two cultures, each with different beliefs and value systems. And much of his life, he stuttered and had difficulty communicating effectively.

After saving the life of an Israelite by killing his Egyptian attacker, Moses became a wanted man and had to flee his homeland. Though he married and fathered children, he nearly lost his life when he delayed circumcising one of his sons. Then, when he undertook his Divinely ordained mission, he found that his task was seemingly impossible and thankless. He was verbally attacked by the pharaoh and by his own people on numerous occasions. And finally, after reaching the pinnacle of religious experience atop Mount Sinai, Moses was excommunicated for a time by the Divine Presence.

We might think that after someone has experienced Divine revelation, life would be simple and sweet. We might imagine that some quietude of the soul results from this very lofty type of experience and existence. However, just the opposite is usually true. Grappling with issues deep in our psyche lets other thoughts that lie deep within us rise to the surface. So, rather than becoming serene, we are often challenged along our journey. We discover that we are at a distance from the community of which we are a part. We are no longer in the same place as others around us. We may feel alone and misunderstood, even when surrounded by family and friends. However, no matter where we are on our own personal journey, we can consciously try to face whatever challenges we encounter. We can choose to find our own path to self-knowledge, self-fulfillment, and self-actualization.

Know that you contain a spark of the Divine.

Even as a baby, Moses's face radiated in a special manner. And the image of the adult Moses that has been passed down through generations is of a man radiating beams of light as he descended from Mount Sinai, carrying the tablets of the Law. His face reflected the Divine light that he had encountered atop the mountain.

Each of us is blessed with an inner light, a spark of the Divine. The more that we walk in God's ways and spend our lives trying to become closer to God, the more we become fully alive. We can become larger than life and connect with eternity. We are capable of achieving our own levels of radiance, our own charisma. And by acting in accordance with the ways of God, we have the opportunity to transmit our own light to others.

Acknowledge your humanity.

No matter how great he was, or how many Divine revelations he was privy to, Moses remained a human being, like the rest of us. And being human, he had doubts, just as we do. Remember that at one crucial point in history, his doubts actually caused him to delay performing a ritual circumcision—symbolic of the covenant with Abraham—on his newborn son. On another occasion, Moses was excommunicated by God when he was ordered to "go down" from Mount Sinai as his followers engaged in idolatry and immorality around the golden calf.

Yet, with all of the difficulties and setbacks that he faced, Moses ultimately enjoyed the most intimate relationship that we can achieve with God. Each of us will also encounter many doubts and frustrations on our own journeys through life. But we need not fear such thoughts. We can recognize them as part of the human condition as we struggle with them and strive to go further in our own search for spiritual growth.

Have an ongoing dialogue with God.

Many people I know pray on a regular basis, some several times a day. And patients whom I meet—particularly those about to undergo surgery—pray quite fervently. Yet, often, their prayers seem to be one-way conversations or wish lists rather than true dialogues. Many of us have been raised to believe that only words from a prayer book can be recited at particular times. Occasionally, someone asks me, "What is the appropriate liturgy to recite when you visit a terminally ill patient?" The answer is, "There is no one fixed text." What occurs during each of my pastoral visits obviously depends on where a particular individual is—physically, emotionally, and spiritually—at that moment in his or her life. Just as we saw when Moses pleaded with God not to let Divine wrath consume the people, we can utilize our partnership with God to influence Divine actions. Even by merely articulating our prayers, we can sometimes hear—with our inner ear—how to go forward.

My friend Elizabeth beautifully described how, by transforming her prayers into a dialogue, she achieved new spiritual insights. One day in class, we discussed God's "loneliness"—how God seeks out humans to be partners in the ongoing task of creating the world. The next Friday, as Elizabeth prepared to light her Sabbath candles, she put aside her mental list of needs that had been on her mind throughout the week. Instead, as she kindled the lights, Elizabeth turned her attention to God and wished God a "Good Sabbath." In that moment, her entire approach to the Sabbath completely turned around, and she found the peace that is the real goal of that day.

Know that your relationship with God is reciprocal.

Our relationship with God is always reciprocal. We want God to be attuned to our needs and prayers, but at the same time, we should be attuned to God. For, after all, our relationship with the Divine is, ideally, based on love.

In every loving relationship, we tend to reflect the feelings of the ones who are dear to us. When a close friend or relative is depressed, anxious, or upset, we are also, to some extent, depressed, anxious, or upset. And the reverse is also true.

Some years ago, it was my good fortune to know a local leader, Robert, who was the guiding force behind many of the finest charitable institutions in Los Angeles. He was strong and purposeful, yet also kind and gentle, and he knew how to get things done quickly and efficiently. He dressed well, walked quickly, and possessed a kind of charisma. You always knew when he was around. His effect on others was so great that it extended beyond his mere physical presence. One day, the wife of a colleague told me, "I can always tell when Robert has stopped by the office to see my husband. When my guy comes home at the end of the day, he's a totally changed man!"

It is clear that we have an effect on one another. Similarly, our closeness to God will lead to our own transformation.

Take the initiative to meet God—
and God will meet you halfway.

As we saw during the giving of the Ten Commandments, two actions occurred simultaneously. As Moses ascended the mountain, God descended to come closer to humanity. This same expression of God's going down is used numerous times when the Bible describes Divine revelation. It represents the union of divinity and humanity.

This concept of movement is instructive for all of us. In any loving relationship, we cannot wait for the other party to take the first step. We must each take the initiative in approaching the other. And this truth does not apply only when making amends. For example, the process of healing is not a one-sided affair. However, many patients regard it as such when they approach a physician with the expectation that he or she will provide some sort of miraculous cure. They hope that by swallowing one magical pill, all their bothersome symptoms will disappear.

But the physician will often say, "You've got to lose some weight and exercise more" or "reduce your salt intake," or "cut back on your work schedule," or "quit smoking." At that point, it is up to the patient to take the initiative—to move in the right direction without waiting passively for the cure to take place.

The idea of going out to meet the other is also one of the most accurate depictions of true love. Two beings who are destined to love each other may feel a mutual attraction as they glimpse each other from afar and move toward each other simultaneously. Two friends who are dear to me, whose courtship was very romantic, used this idea as the theme of their wedding. Their marriage souvenirs were inscribed with the phrase: "As I went out toward you, so I found you coming toward me." These words describe the essence of a loving relationship.

Be modest and humble.

We might assume that someone who has been granted Divine revelation and chosen for a holy, unique mission would feel very important, perhaps even haughty. But throughout Moses's life, his ego remained remarkably uninflated. He demonstrated that he regarded his mission as simply what he did in life. He did not see himself as special or all-knowing, but rather, as all too human. He did not jealously guard the gift of prophecy, but on the contrary, he expressed his wish that everyone might share in it. "Would that all the Lord's people were prophets, that the Lord would put His spirit upon them!" His modest, unassuming manner was one of the hallmarks of his greatness and an ideal to which we can all aspire.

Know that you have the ability to transform the Image of God.

As we have seen, Moses's compassionate plea on behalf of his people elicited a remarkable response from God, one that resonates until this day. Now, God would be *"Adonai, Adonai,"* the Eternal One of complete compassion, not the Judge of humanity, as in the past.

God will always remain compassionate, both before people go

astray from the Divine path and afterwards. When things go wrong, Divine compassion will increase, just as ours should.

Perhaps the most helpful advice that I can give is that each of us remember one seemingly simple biblical verse that is the central prayer in Jewish tradition: "Hear, O Israel, the Eternal, our God, the Eternal is one." In effect, that says it all. Any seeming duality in life is, in fact, oneness.

As we proceed along our journey through life, we strive to become closer to God, and ultimately, to emulate God's ways. We can do no better than to pattern our behavior after God's—demonstrating compassion, grace, and mercy to others, and filling our days with acts of loving-kindness.

Moses epitomized this type of existence. I cannot help but think of Moses when I read the beautiful depiction of ideal human behavior that was written by the prophet Micah: "He has told you, O man, what is good; and what does the Lord require of you, but to do justice, and to love kindness, and to walk humbly with your God."

Biblical References

About JEWISH LIGHTS Publishing

People of all faiths and backgrounds yearn for books that attract, engage, educate and spiritually inspire.

Our principal goal is to stimulate thought and help all people learn about who the Jewish People are, where they come from, and what the future can be made to hold. While people of our diverse Jewish heritage are the primary audience, our books speak to people in the Christian world as well and will broaden their understanding of Judaism and the roots of their own faith.

We bring to you authors who are at the forefront of spiritual thought and experience. While each has something different to say, they all say it in a voice that you can hear.

Our books are designed to welcome you and then to engage, stimulate and inspire. We judge our success not only by whether or not our books are beautiful and commercially successful, but by whether or not they make a difference in your life.

We at Jewish Lights take great care to produce beautiful books that present meaningful spiritual content in a form that reflects the art of making high quality books. Therefore, we want to acknowledge those who contributed to the production of this book.

PRODUCTION
Bronwen Battaglia

EDITORIAL & PROOFREADING
Jennifer Goneau & Martha McKinney

COVER DESIGN
Kieran McCabe

COVER/TEXT PRINTING AND BINDING
Lake Book, Melrose Park, Illinois

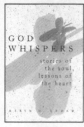

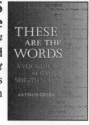

Spirituality

HOW TO BE A PERFECT STRANGER, In 2 Volumes
A Guide to Etiquette in Other People's Religious Ceremonies
Edited by *Stuart M. Matlins & Arthur J. Magida*

BEST REFERENCE BOOK OF THE YEAR

"A book that belongs in every living room, library and office!"

•AWARD WINNER•

Explains the rituals and celebrations of America's major religions/denominations, helping an interested guest to feel comfortable, participate to the fullest extent possible, and avoid violating anyone's religious principles.

Answers practical questions from the perspective of *any* other faith.

VOL. 1: America's Largest Faiths

VOL. 1 COVERS: Assemblies of God • Baptist • Buddhist • Christian Science • Churches of Christ • Disciples of Christ • Episcopalian • Greek Orthodox • Hindu • Islam • Jehovah's Witnesses • Jewish • Lutheran • Methodist • Mormon • Presbyterian • Quaker • Roman Catholic • Seventh-day Adventist • United Church of Christ

6" x 9", 432 pp. Hardcover, ISBN 1-879045-39-7 **$24.95**

VOL. 2: Other Faiths in America

VOL. 2 COVERS: African American Methodist Churches • Baha'i • Christian and Missionary Alliance • Christian Congregation • Church of the Brethren • Church of the Nazarene • Evangelical Free Church of America • International Church of the Foursquare Gospel • International Pentecostal Holiness Church • Mennonite/Amish • Native American • Orthodox Churches • Pentecostal Church of God • Reformed Church of America • Sikh • Unitarian Universalist • Wesleyan

6" x 9", 416 pp. HC, ISBN 1-879045-63-X **$24.95**

GOD & THE BIG BANG
Discovering Harmony Between Science & Spirituality
by *Daniel C. Matt*

Mysticism and science: What do they have in common? How can one enlighten the other? By drawing on modern cosmology and ancient Kabbalah, Matt shows how science and religion can together enrich our spiritual awareness and help us recover a sense of wonder and find our place in the universe.

"This poetic new book...helps us to understand the human meaning of creation."
—*Joel Primack, leading cosmologist, Professor of Physics, University of California, Santa Cruz*

•AWARD WINNER•

6" x 9", 216 pp. Quality Paperback, ISBN 1-879045-89-3 **$16.95**; HC, ISBN-48-6 **$21.95**

MINDING THE TEMPLE OF THE SOUL
Balancing Body, Mind, & Spirit through Traditional Jewish Prayer, Movement, & Meditation
by *Tamar Frankiel* and *Judy Greenfeld*

This new spiritual approach to physical health introduces readers to a spiritual tradition that affirms the body and enables them to reconceive their bodies in a more positive light. Relying on Kabbalistic teachings and other Jewish traditions, it shows us how to be more responsible for our own psychological and physical health. Focuses on the discipline of prayer, simple Tai Chi–like exercises and body positions, and guides the reader throughout, step-by-step, with diagrams, sketches and meditations.

7" x 10", 184 pp. Quality Paperback Original, illus., ISBN 1-879045-64-8 **$16.95**

Audiotape of the Blessings, Movements & Meditations (60-min. cassette) **$9.95**
Videotape of the Movements & Meditations (46-min. VHS) **$20.00**

Spirituality

MEDITATION FROM THE HEART OF JUDAISM
Today's Teachers Share Their Practices, Techniques, and Faith
Edited by *Avram Davis*

A "how-to" guide for both beginning and experienced meditators, it will help you start meditating or help you enhance your practice.

Twenty-two masters of meditation explain why and how they meditate. *A detailed compendium of the experts' "Best Practices"* offers practical advice and starting points.

6" x 9", 256 pp. Quality Paperback, ISBN 1-58023-049-0 **$16.95**
HC, ISBN 1-879045-77-X **$21.95**

SELF, STRUGGLE & CHANGE
Family Conflict Stories in Genesis and Their Healing Insights for Our Lives
by *Norman J. Cohen*

How do I find greater wholeness in my life and in my family's life?

The people described by the biblical writers of Genesis were in situations and relationships very much like our own. We identify with them. Their stories still speak to us because they are about the same problems we deal with every day. Here a modern master of biblical interpretation brings us greater understanding of the ancient text and of ourselves in this intriguing re-telling of conflict between husband and wife, father and son, brothers, and sisters.

6" x 9", 224 pp. Quality Paperback, ISBN 1-879045-66-4 **$16.95**; HC, ISBN-19-2 **$21.95**

VOICES FROM GENESIS
Guiding Us Through the Stages of Life
by *Norman J. Cohen*

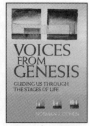

A brilliant blending of modern midrash and the life stages of Erik Erikson's developmental psychology. Shows how the pathways of our lives are quite similar to those of the leading figures of Genesis who speak directly to us, telling of their spiritual and emotional journeys.

6" x 9", 192 pp. HC, ISBN 1-879045-75-3 **$21.95**

ISRAEL—A SPIRITUAL TRAVEL GUIDE
A Companion for the Modern Jewish Pilgrim
by *Rabbi Lawrence A. Hoffman*

Be spiritually prepared for your journey to Israel.

A Jewish spiritual travel guide to Israel, helping today's pilgrim tap into the deep spiritual meaning of the ancient—and modern—sites of the Holy Land. Combines in quick reference format ancient blessings, medieval prayers, biblical and historical references, and modern poetry. The only guidebook that helps readers to prepare spiritually for the occasion. More than a guide book: It is a spiritual map.

4¾" x 10", 256 pp. Quality Paperback Original, ISBN 1-879045-56-7 **$18.95**   •AWARD WINNER•

Spirituality—The Kushner Series

EYES REMADE FOR WONDER
A Lawrence Kushner Reader
Introduction by *Thomas Moore*

A treasury of insight from one of the most creative spiritual thinkers in America. Whether you are new to Kushner or a devoted fan, this is the place to begin. With samplings from each of Kushner's works, and a generous amount of new material, this is a book to be savored, to be read and reread, each time discovering deeper layers of meaning in our lives. Offers something unique to both the spiritual seeker and the committed person of faith.

6" x 9", 240 pp. Quality PB, ISBN 1-58023-042-3 **$16.95**; HC, ISBN -014-8 **$23.95**

INVISIBLE LINES OF CONNECTION
Sacred Stories of the Ordinary
by *Lawrence Kushner*

Through his everyday encounters with family, friends, colleagues and strangers, Kushner takes us deeply into our lives, finding flashes of spiritual insight in the process.

5½" x 8½", 160 pp. Quality Paperback, ISBN 1-879045-98-2 **$15.95**

HC, ISBN -52-4 **$21.95**

•Award Winner•

HONEY FROM THE ROCK
An Easy Introduction to Jewish Mysticism
by *Lawrence Kushner*

"Quite simply the easiest introduction to Jewish mysticism you can read."

An introduction to the ten gates of Jewish mysticism and how it applies to daily life.

6" x 9", 168 pp. Quality Paperback, ISBN 1-879045-02-8 **$14.95**

THE BOOK OF WORDS
Talking Spiritual Life, Living Spiritual Talk
by *Lawrence Kushner*

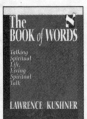

In the incomparable manner of his extraordinary *The Book of Letters*, Kushner now lifts up and shakes the dust off primary religious words we use to describe the spiritual dimension of life. For each word Kushner offers us a startling, moving and insightful explication. He concludes with a short exercise that helps unite the spirit of the word with our actions in the world.

6" x 9", 152 pp. 2-color text, Quality PB ISBN 1-58023-020-2 **$16.95**
HC, ISBN 1-879045-35-4 **$21.95**

THE BOOK OF LETTERS
A Mystical Hebrew Alphabet
by *Lawrence Kushner*

In calligraphy by the author. Folktales about and exploration of the mystical meanings of the Hebrew Alphabet. Draws from ancient Judaic sources, weaving Talmudic commentary, Hasidic folktales, and kabbalistic mysteries around the letters.

• **Popular Hardcover Edition** 6" x 9", 80 pp. HC, two colors, inspiring new Foreword. ISBN 1-879045-00-1 **$24.95**

• **Deluxe Gift Edition** 9" x 12", 80 pp. HC, four-color text, ornamentation, in a beautiful slipcase. **$79.95**

•Award Winner•

• **Collector's Limited Edition** 9" x 12", 80 pp. HC, gold-embossed pages, hand-assembled slipcase. With silkscreened print. **Limited to 500 signed and numbered copies.** ISBN 1-879045-04-4 **$349.00**

Spirituality

GOD WAS IN THIS PLACE & I, i DID NOT KNOW
Finding Self, Spirituality & Ultimate Meaning
by *Lawrence Kushner*

Who am I? Who is God? Kushner creates inspiring interpretations of Jacob's dream in Genesis, opening a window into Jewish spirituality for people of all faiths and backgrounds.

6" x 9", 192 pp. Quality Paperback, ISBN 1-879045-33-8 **$16.95**

THE RIVER OF LIGHT
Spirituality, Judaism, Consciousness
by *Lawrence Kushner*

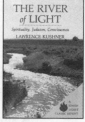

A "manual" for all spiritual travelers who would attempt a spiritual journey in our times. Taking us step by step, Kushner allows us to discover the meaning of our own quest: "to allow the river of light—the deepest currents of consciousness—to rise to the surface and animate our lives."

6" x 9", 180 pp. Quality Paperback, ISBN 1-879045-03-6 **$14.95**

GODWRESTLING—ROUND 2
Ancient Wisdom, Future Paths
by *Arthur Waskow*

This 20th-anniversary sequel to a seminal book of the Jewish renewal movement deals with spirituality in relation to personal growth, marriage, ecology, feminism, politics, and more.

6" x 9", 352 pp. Quality Paperback, ISBN 1-879045-72-9 **$18.95**

HC, ISBN -45-1 **$23.95**

•AWARD WINNER•

ECOLOGY & THE JEWISH SPIRIT
Where Nature & the Sacred Meet
Edited and with Introductions by *Ellen Bernstein*

What is nature's place in our spiritual lives?

A focus on nature is part of the fabric of Jewish thought. Here, experts bring us a richer understanding of the long-neglected themes of nature that are woven through the biblical creation story, ancient texts, traditional law, the holiday cycles, prayer, *mitzvot* (good deeds), and community.

6" x 9", 288 pp. HC, ISBN 1-879045-88-5 **$23.95**

BEING GOD'S PARTNER
How to Find the Hidden Link Between Spirituality and Your Work
by *Jeffrey K. Salkin*; Introduction by *Norman Lear*

Will challenge people of every denomination to reconcile the cares of work and soul. A groundbreaking book about spirituality and the work world, from a Jewish perspective. Offers practical suggestions for balancing your professional life and spiritual self.

6" x 9", 192 pp. Quality Paperback, ISBN 1-879045-65-6 **$16.95**

HC, ISBN -37-0 **$19.95**

Spirituality

MY PEOPLE'S PRAYER BOOK
Traditional Prayers, Modern Commentaries
Vol. 1—The *Sh'ma* and Its Blessings
Vol. 2—The *Amidah*
Vol. 3—*P'sukei D'zimrah* (Morning Psalms)
Edited by *Rabbi Lawrence A. Hoffman*

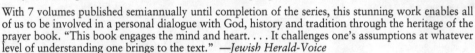

Provides a diverse and exciting commentary to the traditional liturgy, written by 10 of today's most respected scholars and teachers from all perspectives of the Jewish world.

With 7 volumes published semiannually until completion of the series, this stunning work enables all of us to be involved in a personal dialogue with God, history and tradition through the heritage of the prayer book. "This book engages the mind and heart. . . . It challenges one's assumptions at whatever level of understanding one brings to the text." —*Jewish Herald-Voice*

Vol. 1: 7" x 10", 168 pp. HC, ISBN 1-879045-79-6 **$21.95**
Vol. 2: 7" x 10", 240 pp. HC, ISBN 1-879045-80-X **$21.95**
Vol. 3: 7" x 10", 192 pp. (est.) HC, ISBN 1-879045-81-8 **$21.95**

FINDING JOY
A Practical Spiritual Guide to Happiness
by *Dannel I. Schwartz* with *Mark Hass*

Searching for happiness in our modern world of stress and struggle is common; *finding* it is more unusual. This guide explores and explains how to find joy through a time-honored, creative—and surprisingly practical—approach based on the teachings of Jewish mysticism and Kabbalah.

"Lovely, simple introduction to Kabbalah....a singular contribution...."
—*American Library Association's* Booklist

•AWARD WINNER•
6" x 9", 192 pp. Quality PB, ISBN 1-58023-009-1 **$14.95** HC, ISBN 1-879045-53-2 **$19.95**

THE DEATH OF DEATH
Resurrection and Immortality in Jewish Thought
by *Neil Gillman*

Explores the original and compelling argument that Judaism, a religion often thought to pay little attention to the afterlife, not only offers us rich ideas on the subject—but delivers a deathblow to death itself.

6" x 9", 336 pp., HC, ISBN 1-879045-61-3 **$23.95**

THE EMPTY CHAIR: FINDING HOPE & JOY
Timeless Wisdom from a Hasidic Master,
Rebbe Nachman of Breslov
Adapted by *Moshe Mykoff* and the *Breslov Research Institute*

A "little treasure" of aphorisms and advice for living joyously and spiritually today, written 200 years ago, but startlingly fresh in meaning and use.
Teacher, guide and spiritual master—Rebbe Nachman provides vital words of inspiration and wisdom for life today for people of any faith, or of no faith.

•AWARD WINNER• "For anyone of any faith, this is a book of healing and wholeness, of being alive!"
— *Bookviews*
4" x 6", 128 pp., 2-color text, Deluxe Paperback, ISBN 1-879045-67-2 **$9.95**

THE GENTLE WEAPON
Prayers for Everyday and Not-So-Everyday Moments
Adapted by *Moshe Mykoff* and *S.C. Mizrahi*,
together with the *Breslov Research Institute*

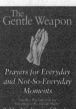

A small treasury of prayers for people of all faiths, based on the Jewish wisdom tradition. The perfect companion to *The Empty Chair: Finding Hope and Joy*, and to our stressful lives.

4" x 6", 144 pp., 2-color text, Deluxe Paperback, ISBN 1-58023-022-9 **$9.95**

Theology/Philosophy

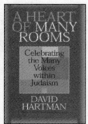

A HEART OF MANY ROOMS
Celebrating the Many Voices within Judaism
by *David Hartman*

With clarity, passion and outstanding scholarship, David Hartman addresses the spiritual and theological questions that face all Jews and all people today. From the perspective of traditional Judaism, he helps us understand the varieties of 20th-century Jewish practice and shows that commitment to both Jewish tradition and to pluralism can create bridges of understanding between people of different religious convictions.

"An extraordinary book, devoid of stereotypic thinking; lucid and pertinent, a modern classic."
—*Michael Walzer, Institute for Advanced Study, Princeton*

6" x 9", 352 pp. HC, ISBN 1-58023-048-2 **$24.95**

**WINNER,
National Jewish
Book Award**

A LIVING COVENANT
The Innovative Spirit in Traditional Judaism
by *David Hartman*

The Judaic tradition is often seen as being more concerned with uncritical obedience to law than with individual freedom and responsibility. Hartman challenges this approach by revealing a Judaism grounded in a covenant—a relational framework— informed by the metaphor of marital love rather than that of parent-child dependency.

"Jews and non-Jews, liberals and traditionalists will see classic Judaism anew
in these pages."   —*Dr. Eugene B. Borowitz,
Hebrew Union College–Jewish Institute of Religion*   •AWARD WINNER•

6" x 9", 368 pp. Quality Paperback, ISBN 1-58023-011-3 **$18.95**

• CLASSICS BY ABRAHAM JOSHUA HESCHEL •

The Earth Is the Lord's: The Inner World of the Jew in Eastern Europe
5½" x 8", 112 pp, Quality Paperback, ISBN 1-879045-42-7 **$13.95**

Israel: An Echo of Eternity with new Introduction by Susannah Heschel
5½" x 8", 272 pp, Quality Paperback, ISBN 1-879045-70-2 **$18.95**

A Passion for Truth: Despair and Hope in Hasidism
5½" x 8", 352 pp, Quality Paperback, ISBN 1-879045-41-9 **$18.95**

• THEOLOGY & PHILOSOPHY...Other books•

Aspects of Rabbinic Theology by Solomon Schechter, with a new Introduction
by Neil Gillman 6" x 9", 440 pp, Quality Paperback, ISBN 1-879045-24-9 **$18.95**

*The Last Trial: On the Legends and Lore of the Command to Abraham to Offer
Isaac as a Sacrifice* by Shalom Spiegel, with a new Introduction by Judah Goldin
6" x 9", 208 pp, Quality Paperback, ISBN 1-879045-29-X **$17.95**

Judaism and Modern Man: An Interpretation of Jewish Religion by Will Herberg; new
Introduction by Neil Gillman 5½" x 8½", 336 pp, Quality Paperback, ISBN 1-879045-87-7 **$18.95**

*Seeking the Path to Life: Theological Meditations On God and the Nature of
People, Love, Life and Death* by Rabbi Ira F. Stone
6" x 9", 132 pp, Quality Paperback, ISBN 1-879045-47-8 **$14.95**; HC, ISBN 1-879045-17-6 **$19.95**

The Spirit of Renewal: Finding Faith After the Holocaust by Edward Feld
6" x 9", 224 pp, Quality Paperback, ISBN 1-879045-40-0 **$16.95**

Tormented Master: The Life and Spiritual Quest of Rabbi Nahman of Bratslav
by Arthur Green 6" x 9", 408 pp, Quality Paperback, ISBN 1-879045-11-7 **$18.95**

Your Word Is Fire Ed. and trans. with a new Introduction by Arthur Green and
Barry W. Holtz 6" x 9", 152 pp, Quality Paperback, ISBN 1-879045-25-7 **$14.95**

Healing/Recovery/Wellness

Experts Praise *Twelve Jewish Steps to Recovery*

"Recommended reading for people of all denominations."
—*Rabbi Abraham J. Twerski, M.D.*

TWELVE JEWISH STEPS TO RECOVERY
A Personal Guide to Turning from Alcoholism & Other Addictions...Drugs, Food, Gambling, Sex...
by *Rabbi Kerry M. Olitzky & Stuart A. Copans, M.D.*
Preface by *Abraham J. Twerski, M.D.*; Intro. by *Rabbi Sheldon Zimmerman*; "Getting Help" by *JACS Foundation*

A Jewish perspective on the Twelve Steps of addiction recovery programs with consolation, inspiration and motivation for recovery. It draws from traditional sources and quotes from what recovering Jewish people say about their experiences with addictions of all kinds. Inspiring illustrations of the twelve gates of the Old City of Jerusalem introduce each step.

6" x 9", 136 pp. Quality Paperback, ISBN 1-879045-09-5 **$13.95**

Recovery from Codependence: A Jewish Twelve Steps Guide to Healing Your Soul
by Rabbi Kerry M. Olitzky

6" x 9", 160 pp. Quality Paperback Original, ISBN 1-879045-32-X **$13.95**; HC, ISBN -27-3 **$21.95**

Renewed Each Day: Daily Twelve Step Recovery Meditations Based on the Bible
by Rabbi Kerry M. Olitzky & Aaron Z.

6" x 9", Quality Paperback Original **V. I**, 224 pp., ISBN 1-879045-12-5 **$14.95**
V. II, 280 pp., ISBN 1-879045-13-3 **$16.95**

One Hundred Blessings Every Day: Daily Twelve Step Recovery Affirmations, Exercises for Personal Growth & Renewal Reflecting Seasons of the Jewish Year
by Rabbi Kerry M. Olitzky

4½" x 6½", 432 pp. Quality Paperback Original, ISBN 1-879045-30-3 **$14.95**

HEALING OF SOUL, HEALING OF BODY
Spiritual Leaders Unfold the Strength and Solace in Psalms
Edited by *Rabbi Simkha Y. Weintraub, CSW, for The Jewish Healing Center*

A source of solace for those who are facing illness, as well as those who care for them. The ten Psalms which form the core of this healing resource were originally selected 200 years ago by Rabbi Nachman of Breslov as a "complete remedy." Today, for anyone coping with illness, they continue to provide a wellspring of strength. Each Psalm is newly translated, making it clear and accessible, and each one is introduced by an eminent rabbi, men and women reflecting different movements and backgrounds. To all who are living with the pain and uncertainty of illness, this spiritual resource offers an anchor of spiritual comfort.

"Will bring comfort to anyone fortunate enough to read it. This gentle book is
a luminous gem of wisdom."
—*Larry Dossey, M.D., author of* Healing Words: The Power
of Prayer & the Practice of Medicine

6" x 9", 128 pp. Quality Paperback Original, illus., 2-color text, ISBN 1-879045-31-1 **$14.95**

Life Cycle

GRIEF IN OUR SEASONS
A Mourner's Kaddish Companion
by *Rabbi Kerry M. Olitzky*

Strength from the Jewish tradition for the first year of mourning.

Provides a wise and inspiring selection of sacred Jewish writings and a simple, powerful ancient ritual for mourners to read each day, to help hold the memory of their loved ones in their hearts. It offers a comforting, step-by-step daily link to saying *Kaddish*.

"A hopeful, compassionate guide along the journey from grief to rebirth from mourning to a new morning."
— *Rabbi Levi Meier, Ph.D., Chaplain, Cedars–Sinai Medical Center, Los Angeles*

4½" x 6½", 448 pp. Quality Paperback Original, ISBN 1-879045-55-9 **$15.95**

MOURNING & MITZVAH   • WITH OVER 60 GUIDED EXERCISES •
A Guided Journal for Walking the Mourner's Path Through Grief to Healing
by *Anne Brener, L.C.S.W.*
Foreword by *Rabbi Jack Riemer*; Introduction by *Rabbi William Cutter*

"Fully engaging in mourning means you will be a different person than before you began." **For those who mourn a death, for those who would help them,** for those who face a loss of any kind, Brener teaches us the power and strength available to us in the fully experienced mourning process. Guided writing exercises help stimulate the processes of both conscious and unconscious healing.

"A stunning book! It offers an exploration in depth of the place where psychology and religious ritual intersect, and the name of that place is Truth."
— *Rabbi Harold Kushner, author of* When Bad Things Happen to Good People

7½" x 9", 288 pp. Quality Paperback Original, ISBN 1-879045-23-0 **$19.95**

A TIME TO MOURN, A TIME TO COMFORT
A Guide to Jewish Bereavement and Comfort
by *Dr. Ron Wolfson*

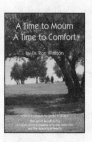

A guide to meeting the needs of those who mourn and those who seek to provide comfort in times of sadness. While this book is written from a layperson's point of view, it also includes the specifics for funeral preparations and practical guidance for preparing the home and family to sit *shiva*.

"A sensitive and perceptive guide to Jewish tradition. Both those who mourn and those who comfort will find it a map to accompany them through the whirlwind."
— *Deborah E. Lipstadt, Emory University*

7" x 9", 336 pp. Quality Paperback, ISBN 1-879045-96-6 **$16.95**

WHEN A GRANDPARENT DIES
A Kid's Own Remembering Workbook for Dealing with Shiva and the Year Beyond
by *Nechama Liss-Levinson, Ph.D.*

Drawing insights from both psychology and Jewish tradition, this workbook helps children participate in the process of mourning, offering guided exercises, rituals, and places to write, draw, list, create and express their feelings.

"Will bring support, guidance, and understanding for countless children, teachers, and health professionals."
— *Rabbi Earl A. Grollman, D.D., author of* Talking about Death

8" x 10", 48 pp. HC, illus., 2-color text, ISBN 1-879045-44-3 **$15.95**

Art of Jewish Living Series for Holiday Observance

THE SHABBAT SEDER
by *Dr. Ron Wolfson*

A concise step-by-step guide designed to teach people the meaning and importance of this weekly celebration, as well as its practices.

Each chapter corresponds to one of ten steps which together comprise the Shabbat dinner ritual, and looks at the *concepts, objects,* and *meanings* behind the specific activity or ritual act. The blessings that accompany the meal are written in both Hebrew and English, and accompanied by English transliteration. Also included are craft projects, recipes, discussion ideas and other creative suggestions for enriching the Shabbat experience.

"A how-to book in the best sense...."
—*Dr. David Lieber, President, University of Judaism, Los Angeles*

7" x 9", 272 pp. Quality Paperback, ISBN 1-879045-90-7 **$16.95**

Also available are these helpful companions to *The Shabbat Seder*:
- •Booklet of the Blessings and Songs   ISBN 1-879045-91-5 $5.00
- •Audiocassette of the Blessings   DNO3 $6.00
- •Teacher's Guide   ISBN 1-879045-92-3 $4.95

HANUKKAH
by *Dr. Ron Wolfson*
Edited by *Joel Lurie Grishaver*

Designed to help celebrate and enrich the holiday season, *Hanukkah* discusses the holiday's origins, explores the reasons for the Hanukkah candles and customs, and provides everything from recipes to family activities.

There are songs, recipes, useful information on the arts and crafts of Hanukkah, the calendar and its relationship to Christmas time, and games played at Hanukkah. Putting the holiday in a larger, timely context, "December Dilemmas" deals with ways in which a Jewish family can cope with Christmas.

"Helpful for the family that strives to induct its members into the spirituality and joys of Jewishness and Judaism...a significant text in the neglected art of Jewish family education."
—*Rabbi Harold M. Schulweis, Cong. Valley Beth Shalom, Encino, CA*

7" x 9", 192 pp. Quality Paperback, ISBN 1-879045-97-4 **$16.95**

THE PASSOVER SEDER
by *Dr. Ron Wolfson*

Explains the concepts behind Passover ritual and ceremony in clear, easy-to-understand language, and offers step-by-step procedures for Passover observance and preparing the home for the holiday.

Easy-to-Follow Format: Using an innovative photo-documentary technique, real families describe in vivid images their own experiences with the Passover holiday.
Easy-to-Read Hebrew Texts: The Haggadah texts in Hebrew, English, and transliteration are presented in a three-column format designed to help celebrants learn the meaning of the prayers and how to read them.
An Abundance of Useful Information: A detailed description of how to perform the rituals is included, along with practical questions and answers, and imaginative ideas for Seder celebration.

"A creative 'how-to' for making the Seder a more meaningful experience."
—*Michael Strassfeld, co-author of* The Jewish Catalog

7" x 9", 336 pp. Quality Paperback, ISBN 1-879045-93-1 **$16.95**

Also available are these helpful companions to *The Passover Seder*:
- •Passover Workbook   ISBN 1-879045-94-X $6.95
- •Audiocassette of the Blessings   DNO4 $6.00
- •Teacher's Guide   ISBN 1-879045-95-8 $4.95

Life Cycle

TEARS OF SORROW, SEEDS OF HOPE
A Jewish Spiritual Companion for Infertility and Pregnancy Loss
by *Rabbi Nina Beth Cardin*

Many people who endure the emotional suffering of infertility, pregnancy loss, or stillbirth bear this sorrow alone. Rarely is the experience of loss and infertility discussed with anyone but close friends and family members. Despite the private nature of the pain, many women and men would welcome the opportunity to be comforted by family and a community who would understand the pain and loneliness they feel, and the emptiness caused by the loss that is without a face, a name, or a grave.

Tears of Sorrow, Seeds of Hope is a spiritual companion that enables us to mourn infertility, a lost pregnancy, or a stillbirth within the prayers, rituals, and meditation of Judaism. By drawing deeply on the texts of tradition, it creates readings and rites of mourning, and through them provides a wellspring of compassion, solace—and hope.

6" x 9", 192 pp. HC, ISBN 1-58023-017-2 **$19.95**

LIFECYCLES

V. 1: Jewish Women on Life Passages & Personal Milestones
Edited and with Introductions by *Rabbi Debra Orenstein*
V. 2: Jewish Women on Biblical Themes in Contemporary Life
Edited and with Introductions by
Rabbi Debra Orenstein and *Rabbi Jane Rachel Litman*

This unique multivolume collaboration brings together over one hundred women writers, rabbis, and scholars to create the first comprehensive work on Jewish life cycle that fully includes women's perspectives.

V. 1: 6" x 9", 480 pp. Quality Paperback, ISBN 1-58023-018-0 **$19.95**
HC, ISBN 1-879045-14-1 **$24.95**

V. 2: 6" x 9", 464 pp. Quality Paperback, ISBN 1-58023-019-9 **$19.95**
HC, ISBN 1-879045-15-X **$24.95**

•AWARD WINNER•

LIFE CYCLE— The Art of Jewish Living Series for Holiday Observance
by Dr. Ron Wolfson

Hanukkah—7" x 9", 192 pp. Quality Paperback, ISBN 1-879045-97-4 **$16.95**

The Shabbat Seder—7" x 9", 272 pp. Quality Paperback, ISBN 1-879045-90-7 **$16.95**;
Booklet of Blessings **$5.00**; Audiocassette of Blessings **$6.00**; Teacher's Guide **$4.95**

The Passover Seder—7" x 9", 336 pp. Quality Paperback, ISBN 1-879045-93-1 **$16.95**;
Passover Workbook, **$6.95**; Audiocassette of Blessings, **$6.00**; Teacher's Guide, **$4.95**

• LIFE CYCLE...Other Books •

A Heart of Wisdom: Making the Jewish Journey from Midlife Through the Elder Years
Ed. by Susan Berrin 6" x 9", 384 pp. Quality Paperback, ISBN 1-58023-051-2, **$18.95**;
HC, ISBN 1-879045-73-7 **$24.95**

Bar/Bat Mitzvah Basics: A Practical Family Guide to Coming of Age Together
Ed. by Cantor Helen Leneman 6" x 9", 240 pp. Quality Paperback, ISBN 1-879045-54-0 **$16.95**

Embracing the Covenant: Converts to Judaism Talk About Why & How
Ed. and with Intros. by Rabbi Allan L. Berkowitz and Patti Moskovitz
6" x 9", 192 pp. Quality Paperback, ISBN 1-879045-50-8 **$15.95**

For Kids—Putting God on Your Guest List: How to Claim the Spiritual Meaning of Your Bar or Bat Mitzvah by Rabbi Jeffrey K. Salkin
6" x 9", 144 pp. Quality Paperback Original, ISBN 1-58023-015-6 **$14.95**

The New Jewish Baby Book: Names, Ceremonies, Customs—A Guide for Today's Families by Anita Diamant 6" x 9", 336 pp. Quality Paperback, ISBN 1-879045-28-1 **$16.95**

Putting God on the Guest List, 2nd Ed.: How to Reclaim the Spiritual Meaning of Your Child's Bar or Bat Mitzvah by Rabbi Jeffrey K. Salkin
6" x 9", 224 pp. Quality Paperback, ISBN 1-897045-59-1 **$16.95**; HC, ISBN 1-879045-58-3 **$24.95**

So That Your Values Live On: Ethical Wills & How to Prepare Them
Ed. by Rabbi Jack Riemer & Professor Nathaniel Stampfer
6" x 9", 272 pp. Quality Paperback, ISBN 1-879045-34-6 **$17.95**

Children's Spirituality

A PRAYER FOR THE EARTH
The Story of Naamah, Noah's Wife

For ages 4 and up

by *Sandy Eisenberg Sasso*

Full-color illustrations by *Bethanne Andersen*

NONDENOMINATIONAL, NONSECTARIAN

This new story, based on an ancient text, opens readers' religious imaginations to new ideas about the well-known story of the Flood. When God tells Noah to bring the animals of the world onto the ark, God *also* calls on Naamah, Noah's wife, to save each plant on Earth.

"A lovely tale....Children of all ages should be drawn to this parable for our times."

•AWARD WINNER•

—*Tomie dePaola, artist/author of books for children*

9" x 12", 32 pp. HC, Full-color illus., ISBN 1-879045-60-5 **$16.95**

THE 11TH COMMANDMENT
Wisdom from Our Children

For all ages

by The Children of America

MULTICULTURAL, NONDENOMINATIONAL, NONSECTARIAN

"If there were an Eleventh Commandment, what would it be?"

Children of many religious denominations across America answer this question—in their own drawings and words—in *The 11th Commandment*.

"Wonderful....This unusual book provides both food for thought and insight into the hopes and fears of today's young."
—*American Library Association's* Booklist

8" x 10", 48 pp. HC, Full-color illus., ISBN 1-879045-46-X **$16.95**

SHARING BLESSINGS
Children's Stories for Exploring the Spirit of the Jewish Holidays

For ages 6 and up

by *Rahel Musleah* and *Rabbi Michael Klayman*

Full-color illustrations by *Mary O'Keefe Young*

What is the spiritual message of each of the Jewish holidays? How do we teach it to our children?

Many books tell children about the historical significance and customs of the holidays. Now, through engaging, creative stories about one family's spiritual preparation, *Sharing Blessings* explores ways to get into the *spirit* of 13 different holidays.

"A beguiling introduction to important Jewish values by way of the holidays."
—*Rabbi Harold Kushner, author of* When Bad Things Happen to Good People *and* How Good Do We Have to Be?

7" x 10", 64 pp. HC, Full-color illus., ISBN 1-879045-71-0 **$18.95**

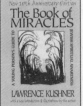

THE BOOK OF MIRACLES
A Young Person's Guide to Jewish Spiritual Awareness

For ages 9–13

by *Lawrence Kushner*

With a Special 10th Anniversary Introduction and all new illustrations by the author.

From the miracle at the Red Sea to the miracle of waking up this morning, this intriguing book introduces kids to a way of everyday spiritual thinking to last a lifetime. Kushner, whose award-winning books have brought spirituality to life for countless adults, now shows young people how to use Judaism as a foundation on which to build their lives.

6" x 9", 96 pp. HC, 2-color illus., ISBN 1-879045-78-8 **$16.95**

Children's Spirituality

For ages 8 and up

BUT GOD REMEMBERED
Stories of Women from Creation to the Promised Land
by *Sandy Eisenberg Sasso*, Full-color illus. by *Bethanne Andersen*

NONDENOMINATIONAL, NONSECTARIAN

A fascinating collection of four different stories of women only briefly mentioned in biblical tradition and religious texts, but never before explored. Award-winning author Sasso brings to life the intriguing stories of Lilith, Serach, Bityah, and the Daughters of Z, courageous and strong women from ancient tradition. All teach important values through their faith and actions.

9" x 12", 32 pp. HC, Full-color illus., ISBN 1-879045-43-5 **$16.95**

•AWARD WINNER•

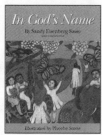

IN GOD'S NAME
by *Sandy Eisenberg Sasso*

For ages 4 and up

Selected as Outstanding by Parent Council, Ltd.™

Full-color illustrations by *Phoebe Stone*

MULTICULTURAL, NONDENOMINATIONAL, NONSECTARIAN

Like an ancient myth in its poetic text and vibrant illustrations, this modern fable about the search for God's name celebrates the diversity and, at the same time, the unity of all the people of the world. Each seeker claims he or she alone knows the answer. Finally, they come together and learn what God's name really is, sharing the ultimate harmony of belief in one God by people of all faiths, all backgrounds.

•AWARD WINNER•

9" x 12", 32 pp. HC, Full color illus., ISBN 1-879045-26-5 **$16.95**

For ages 4 and up

GOD IN BETWEEN

by *Sandy Eisenberg Sasso*
Full-color illustrations by *Sally Sweetland*

NONDENOMINATIONAL, NONSECTARIAN, MULTICULTURAL

If you wanted to find God, where would you look?

A magical, mythical tale that teaches that God can be found where we are: within all of us and the relationships between us.

9" x 12", 32 pp. HC, Full-color illus., ISBN 1-879045-86-9 **$16.95**

IN OUR IMAGE
God's First Creatures

For ages 4 and up

by *Nancy Sohn Swartz*

Selected as Outstanding by Parent Council, Ltd.™

Full-color illustrations by *Melanie Hall*
NONDENOMINATIONAL, NONSECTARIAN
For ages 4 and up

A playful new twist to the Creation story. Celebrates the interconnectedness of nature and the harmony of all living things.

9" x 12", 32 pp. HC, Full-color illus., ISBN 1-879045-99-0 **$16.95**

•AWARD WINNER•

•AWARD WINNER•

For ages 4 and up

GOD'S PAINTBRUSH
by *Sandy Eisenberg Sasso*
Full-color illustrations by *Annette Compton*

MULTICULTURAL, NONDENOMINATIONAL, NONSECTARIAN

Invites children of all faiths and backgrounds to encounter God openly in their own lives. Wonderfully interactive, provides questions adult and child can explore together at the end of each episode.

11" x 8½", 32 pp. HC, Full-color illus., ISBN 1-879045-22-2 **$16.95**

Also Available! **Teacher's Guide: A Guide for Jewish & Christian Educators and Parents**
8½" x 11", 32 pp. PB, ISBN 1-879045-57-5 **$6.95**

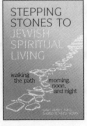

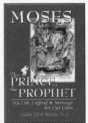